Scot Ober
Ball State University

Jack E. Johnson
State University of West Georgia

Arlene Zimmerly
Los Angeles City College

Visit the *College Keyboarding* Web site at www.mhhe.com/gdp

Boston   Burr Ridge, IL   Dubuque, IA   Madison, WI   New York   San Francisco   St. Louis
Bangkok   Bogotá   Caracas   Kuala Lumpur   Lisbon   London   Madrid   Mexico City
Milan   Montreal   New Delhi   Santiago   Seoul   Singapore   Sydney   Taipei   Toronto

McGraw-Hill/Irwin Technical Support

Thank you for purchasing this McGraw-Hill software product. McGraw-Hill/Irwin is dedicated to providing you with the highest quality software and ensuring that you receive the finest technical support for products you purchase.

To help support our customers, we register all of our software users. To become a registered user, complete the registration card that was included with your software and send it to McGraw-Hill/Irwin.

Telephone support for all registered users is available between 8 A.M. and 5 P.M. (CST) at 1-800-331-5094. Customers with specific questions can e-mail software support staff at techsupport@mcgraw-hill.com.

If you have any questions regarding our customer support policy, please e-mail us at the above address or write to us at this address:

McGraw-Hill/Irwin
ATTN: Technical Support
1333 Burr Ridge Parkway
Burr Ridge, IL 60527

This document has been prepared with the help of Dolphin Inc., Voorhees, NJ.

Installation Guide for GDP10 Campus Software for use with
COLLEGE KEYBOARDING & DOCUMENT PROCESSING
Scot Ober, Jack E. Johnson, Arlene Zimmerly

Published by McGraw-Hill/Irwin, an imprint of The McGraw-Hill Companies, Inc., 1221 Avenue of the Americas, New York, NY 10020. Copyright © 2006 by The McGraw-Hill Companies, Inc. All rights reserved.

No part of this publication may be reproduced or distributed in any form or by any means, or stored in a database or retrieval system, without the prior written consent of The McGraw-Hill Companies, Inc., including, but not limited to, in any network or other electronic storage or transmission, or broadcast for distance learning.

Microsoft® and MS® are registered trademarks, and Windows ™ is a trademark, of Microsoft Corporation.

1 2 3 4 5 6 7 8 9 0 CSS/CSS 0 9 8 7 6 5

ISBN 0-07-305421-6

www.mhhe.com

Contents

Chapter 1: **Getting Started**
1.1 Welcome to GDP 1
    1.1.1 *Features to Help Students Achieve Keyboarding Proficiency*..1
    1.1.2 *Instructor Management's Time-Saving Tools* 1
1.2 GDP Configurations 2
    1.2.1 *Campus Version* 2
    1.2.2 *Home Version* 4
1.3 System Requirements 5
1.4 Required Student Materials...5
1.5 About This Installation Guide..5

Chapter 2: **Installation and Set-Up**
2.1 Overview 6
2.2 Campus with Instructor Management (LAN) Installation and Set-Up........6
    2.2.1 *Install GDP on the Server* 6
    2.2.2 *Set Up Student and Instructor Access to GDP* 10
    2.2.3 *Add New Instructor and Set Up Classes in Instructor Management*.. 11
    2.2.4 *Specify Instructor and Class Settings*........................... 14
    2.2.5 *Register Students into GDP Classes*............................ 17
2.3 Campus without Instructor Management (Standalone) Installation and Set-Up 19
    2.3.1 *Install GDP without Instructor Management on a Standalone Workstation*... 19
    2.3.2 *Specify Settings for the Campus without Instructor Management Configuration* 22
2.4 Set Up The Instructor Management Web Site for Distance Learners 26
2.5 Home Installation and Set-Up..28
    2.5.1 *Install GDP on the Home Computer* 28
    2.5.2 *Set Up the Instructor Management Web Site for (Home) Distance Learners* 30
2.6 About Student Data Files...31
    2.6.1 *Getting Student Data into Instructor Management* 31
    2.6.2 *Changing the Student Data Location* 31
    2.6.3 *Backing up Student Data Files*..................................... 32

Chapter 3: **Using GDP**
    3.1 Logging On 33
        3.1.1 *Logging on to the Campus with Instructor Management (LAN) version* 33
        3.1.2 *Logging on Initially as a Campus without Instructor Management (Standalone) or Distance-Learning Student* 34
        3.1.3 *Logging on as Home Student* 36
    3.2 Working on Lesson Exercises 37
        3.2.1 *Exercise Screen Layout* 39
    3.3 Navigation Menu 40
    3.4 Toolbar 41
    3.5 Drop-Down Menus 42
        3.5.1 *File Menu* 42
        3.5.2 *Options Menu* 43
        3.5.3 *Help Menu* 43
    3.6 Keyboard Shortcuts 44
    3.7 Getting Distance-Learning and Standalone Student Data into Instructor Management 45
        3.7.1 *Sending Distance-Learning Student Data to the Instructor Management Web Site* 45
        3.7.2 *Sending Student Data to the Instructor Management Web Site From Non-MAPI Compliant E-mail* 45
        3.7.3 *Loading Standalone Student Data onto the Instructor Workstation* 45
    3.8 Viewing HTML Versions of Student Work 46

Chapter 4: **Using Instructor Options and Instructor Management**
    4.1 Accessing Instructor Options 47
        4.1.1 *Navigation menu* 48
        4.1.2 *Toolbar* 48
    4.2 About Instructor Management (Gradebook) 49
        4.2.1 *Classes Page* 50
        4.2.2 *Class Summary Report Page* 51

Chapter 5: **Troubleshooting**
    5.1 Installation and Start-Up 53
    5.2 Document Processing and Scoring 55
    5.3 Sound 56
    5.4 E-mail 56
    5.5 Help and Reference Manual 57
    5.6 Instructor Management Program Campus with Instructor Management (LAN) 57
    5.7 Distance Learning/Instructor Management Web Site 57
    5.8 Data Storage Limits 59

Index 60

Chapter 1: Getting Started

1.1 Welcome to GDP

Gregg College Keyboarding & Document Processing (GDP) is a Windows-based program designed for use with the *Gregg College Keyboarding & Document Processing™ 10th Edition* textbook. The software and textbook mirror and reinforce each other. From new key presentations to advanced word processing, all exercises in the textbook are included in one all-encompassing program. For document processing exercises, GDP links to Microsoft Word®.

GDP is designed to work with students on campus as well as at home. Student exercises in GDP are stored in a directory on a network drive, in a local hard-disk directory, or on an external disk.

1.1.1 Features to Help Students Achieve Keyboarding Proficiency

- An intuitive, Web-based interface provides a contemporary learning environment for today's high-tech office and makes it easy for students to use the software even if they have limited computer experience.

- Multimedia "hand" demonstrations for new key presentations allow students to visualize correct finger placement on home row keys while still being able to see all of the keys on the keyboard.

- Interactive language arts tutorials help students build the traditional language arts skills that are essential for effective business communications.

- The MAP (Misstroke Analysis and Prescription) program diagnoses accuracy problems and provides intensive, individualized remediation.

- The tennis game and the pace car game reinforce keyboarding skills in a fun setting.

- Bilingual English/Spanish instruction screens and powerful distance-learning features meet the needs of an increasingly diverse student population.

1.1.2 Instructor Managements' Time-Saving Tools

The Instructor Management program, which works in conjunction with GDP, provides powerful, yet easy-to-use tools for instructors to set up and manage class files, monitor student and class progress, and generate student grades.

- Automatically stores students' work and allows the instructor to view scored text—and add comments.

- Enhances communication with classes: instructors can create and send announcements to classes, send e-mail to individual students, and receive e-mail from students—all from within the GDP software.

- Calculates grades based on the instructor's grading parameters.

- With LAN and Web options, allows instructors to easily manage classes whether they are on or off campus.

1.2 GDP Configurations

GDP is designed to accommodate various instructional needs and computing environments. There are two versions of the software: Campus and Home. Within the Campus version, you have two options for configuring the software and storing and monitoring student work. The Campus version is the one used by schools to install GDP in its various configurations on campus or by a distance- learning instructor off campus. The Home version is the one used by students to work at home as a distance-learning student or under a standalone configuration.

1.2.1 Campus Version

The Campus version of GDP can be installed on a campus-based LAN or on standalone computers on campus in two configurations: With Instructor Management or Without Instructor Management (this configuration denotes that students will either provide instructors with their work manually or upload it to the Instructor Management Web site). Both Campus configurations include the option of Distance-Learning for students (i.e., either a system that has MAPI-compliant e-mail enabled or uses a Student Upload Web site to move data to the Instructor Management Web site). ***Please note that an instructor must have his or her class set up in the Instructor Management Web site in order for the Distance Learning feature to work.*** Where and how you install the Campus version dictates the mechanism for collecting and retrieving student work for Instructor Management.

When you install the Campus with Instructor Management (LAN) version of GDP, you install the GDP and Instructor Management software on the network server. In this configuration, all student data gets stored on the network, which means that you have immediate, seamless access to all student work via the Instructor Management program. Data may also be stored on a floppy disk or other removable media or at a virtual network location—with a copy of student data automatically saved on the network.

How Does the Instructor Access Student Work? In the Campus with Instructor Management (LAN) configuration, all student data is stored in or automatically copied to a central location on the network. The instructor simply logs on to GDP at an instructor workstation and uses the Instructor Management program to monitor student work.

Campus without Instructor Management (Standalone)

When you install the Campus without Instructor Management version of GDP, GDP is installed on a standalone system. Student data is stored on the local hard disk or on a floppy disk or other removable media. The instructor uses the Instructor Management program (on an instructor workstation) to monitor student work, but the process of collecting student data files is manual, not automatic as in the Campus with Instructor Management (LAN) version.

How Does the Instructor Access Student Work? In the Campus without Instructor Management configuration, student data is stored on standalone computers, not centrally. If the instructor wants to use the Instructor Management program to monitor student work, the instructor has to manually collect student data files from individual students and then update the Instructor Management program from those data files. For more information, see 3.7.3 Loading Standalone Student Data onto the Instructor Workstations on page 45.

More Information on Distance Learning in GDP

In order to utilize the Distance-Learning option within GDP's Campus and Home versions, GDP is installed on a system that has MAPI-compliant e-mail enabled (such as Microsoft Outlook® or Outlook Express®) or uses a student upload Web site to move data to the Instructor Management Web site. MAPI, an acronym for Messaging Application Program Interface, enables a Windows application to send e-mail. The MAPI standard provides many benefits, such as the ability to save mail in an "Outbox" for sending later when you are connected to the Internet. The MAPI standard was created by Microsoft and is supported by a number of third-party vendors, including Eudora and Netscape. Microsoft includes MAPI support in e-mail programs such as Outlook Express and Outlook. Many Internet Service Providers (ISPs) provide a MAPI-compliant e-mail program as part of their installed software since they include Microsoft Outlook Express® as the e-mail program. Properly configuring a system for sending e-mail using MAPI requires information from the ISP, such as the address of the ISP's mail server. For this reason, it is not possible to give general instructions for configuring e-mail on any workstation.

Some ISPs, such as America Online (AOL), do not provide a MAPI- compliant e-mail program. If a student is using AOL or is otherwise in a situation where they do not have a MAPI-compliant workstation, the student should use the Export feature in the GDP software to create a file that can be attached to an e-mail and sent to the GDP Instructor Management Web site. It is even possible for a student to use a browser-based e-mail solution (e.g., Hotmail, Yahoo! Mail, Netscape Mail) to send attached files.

For detailed information about MAPI and about the export function, go to the College Keyboarding Web site at www.mhhe.gdp.com and click on the Technical Tips link.

Student data is stored on the local hard disk or a floppy disk. The instructor uses the Instructor Management Web site—rather than the Instructor Management Program—to monitor student work.

How Does the Instructor Access Student Work? When the Distance-Learning option is being used within GDP's Campus version (with or without Instructor Management), student data is stored locally. Periodically, the student uses the Update feature in GDP to send his or her data to the Instructor Management Web site.

4   Chapter 1: Getting Started

1.2.2 Home Version   The Home version allows an individual student to work on GDP off campus. This is a single-user version of GDP, and it can be installed on either a standalone or an e-mail-connected computer.

Home (Standalone)

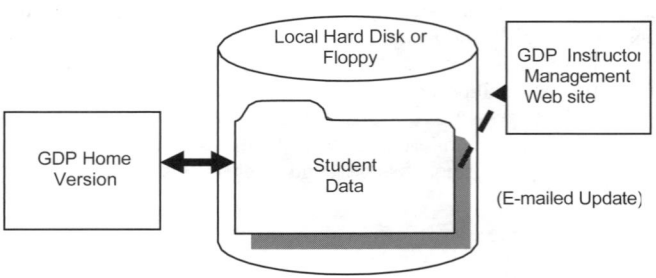

In the Home (Standalone) version, GDP is installed on a standalone off-campus system. Student data is stored on the local hard disk or a floppy disk. Similar to the Campus version, the Home version of GDP includes the option of Distance-Learning for students (i.e., either a system that has MAPI-compliant e-mail enabled or uses a student upload Web site to move data to the Instructor Management Web site). ***Please note that an instructor must have his or her class set up in the Instructor Management Web site in order for the Distance Learning feature to work.*** In this instance, Student Data is updated periodically by the student to the Instructor Management Web site. The instructor uses the Instructor Management Web site – rather than the Instructor Management program – to monitor student work. Please see *'More Information on Distance-Learning in GDP'* on Page 3 for further details regarding MAPI-compliant e-mail protocol.

How Does the Instructor Access Student Work? As in the Campus without Instructor Management configuration, the Home version of GDP requires the instructor to manually collect student data files and then update the Instructor Management program from those data files. See Campus without Instructor Management (Standalone) on Page 3 for information on how to update student data.

When the Distance-Learning option is utilized in the Home version, student data is stored locally. Periodically, the student uses the Update feature in GDP to send his or her data to the Instructor Management Web site.

1.3 System Requirements

To run GDP, your system must meet the following minimum requirements:

- Pentium II CPU or higher

- Microsoft® Windows 98®, NT 4.0®, Me®, 2000®, or XP®

- 16 MB RAM required for Windows 98 system; 32 MB RAM required for Windows NT, 2000, and Me systems; 128 MB RAM required for Windows XP system

- Hard disk drive or network file server with 175 MB of free space

- CD-ROM drive (8X or faster)

- SVGA color monitor that supports 800 x 600 high color or true color resolutions

- Internet connection and either Netscape Navigator 7.0 or Microsoft Internet Explorer 6.0—if distance-learning or Internet features are used

- Microsoft Word 2000, Word 2002, or Word 2003 for document processing exercises

- High-density 3.5" floppy disk drive, if storing student data on floppy disks

- A printer is recommended but not required

- Also recommended: standard audio card compatible with MS Windows MCI

Data will be stored in a student subdirectory on the hard disk, network, or floppy disk for the Campus versions of the program and on the hard disk or a floppy disk for the Home version.

The Instructor Management software resides on a network file server for the Campus with Instructor Management (LAN) version and on the Instructor Management Web site when using the Distance-Learning option in either GDP Campus or Home version. Instructor Management collects and analyzes student data stored on the network file server and on individual floppy disks or other removable media.

1.4 Required Student Materials

To complete instructional activities in the program, students will need the following:
- *Gregg College Keyboarding & Document Processing™, 10th Edition* textbook for the appropriate lessons.

- *Microsoft® Word 2000 Manual for Gregg College Keyboarding& Document Processing, 10th Edition, Lessons 1—120 (or 2002or 2003, depending on your system).*

- Blank disks, if you want your students to store their work on floppy disks or removable media such as a Zip disk.

- Distance-Learning students using GDP at home will need the Home Version of GDP, which is available from McGraw-Hill.

1.5 About This Installation Guide

This Installation Guide is designed to help the instructor or technical support personnel choose the GDP configuration that best meets the instructor's needs, install the GDP software, and set up the GDP software for use by the instructor and students. For detailed information about how GDP or Instructor Management works, see the User's Guide.

Chapter 2: Installation and Set-Up

2.1 Overview

Before installing GDP, you need to decide which configuration best meets your needs. (Refer to 1.2 GDP Configuration on page 2 for detailed information about the various configurations.)

This chapter gives detailed installation and set-up instructions for each configuration (Campus with Instructor Management (LAN), Campus without Instructor Management (Standalone) and Home), taking you through the following general steps:

- Install the GDP software and set up student and instructor access to the software. Depending on your configuration, this entails installing the software on a LAN and on LAN-connected workstations for the Campus with Instructor Management (LAN) configuration, and on standalone computers in a Campus without Instructor Management or Home configuration.

- Set up classes in Instructor Management, if you want to be able to track your students' progress and use the gradebook features in a LAN configuration or on a standalone instructor workstation.

- Set up classes and register students on the Instructor Management Web site, if your students are using the Distance-Learning option available in the various GDP configurations.

- Specify instructor and class settings.

2.2 Campus with Instructor Management (LAN) Installation and Set-Up

2.2.1 Install GDP on the Server

1. Start Windows on a workstation with access to a volume on the network file server.

2. Put the GDP CD-ROM in the workstation's CD-ROM drive.

3. No auto-run.

    a. Open the Start menu (on the Windows task bar) and choose *Run...*

    b. In the Open blank, type **d:\setup** (please note that the CD-ROM drive could be **e:** on some computers). Click **OK**.

4. The InstallShield Wizard loads, then the Welcome dialog box displays. Click **Next** to continue.

5. In the License Agreement dialog box (Figure 2-1), click **I accept**... to accept the terms of the license agreement. Click **Next** to continue. Note: You must accept the license agreement to continue with the installation process.

Chapter 2: Installation and Set-Up 7

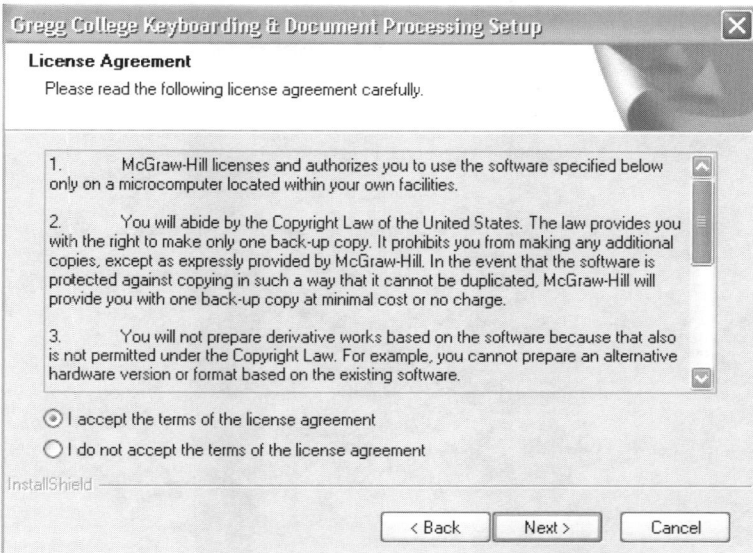

FIGURE 2-1: LICENSE AGREEMENT DIALOG BOX

6. In the Select Components dialog box (Figure 2-2), click **Yes, Install with Instructor Management** to indicate that you are installing GDP on a network server connected to student workstations. Then click **Next**.

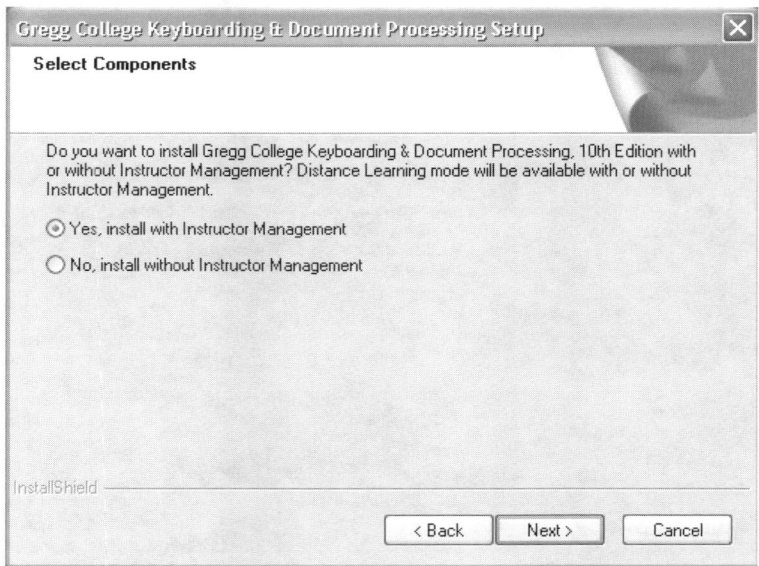

FIGURE 2-2: SELECT COMPONENTS DIALOG BOX

7. In the Select Destination Location dialog box (Figure 2-3), locate the network file server and directory where you want to install the software. Click **Browse** to select a location different from the default. After you select a location, click **Next**.

8 Chapter 2: Installation and Set-Up

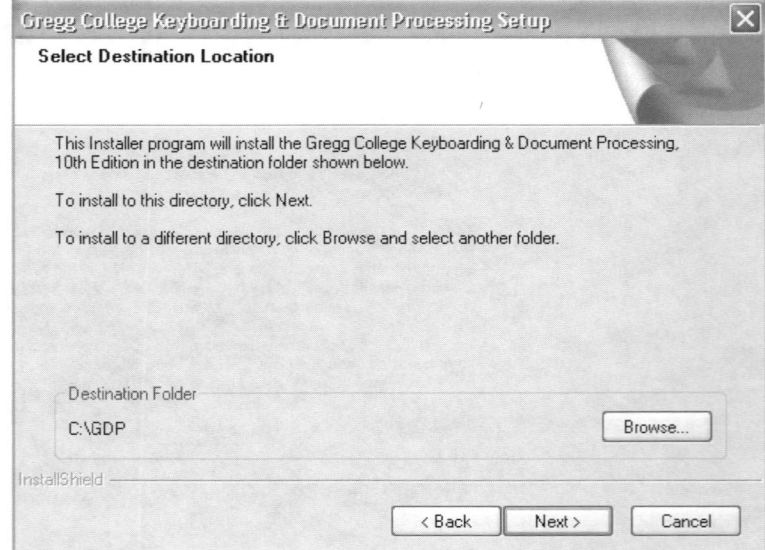

FIGURE 2-3: SELECT DESTINATION LOCATION DIALOG BOX

8. In the Select Class Data Location dialog box (Figure 2-4), locate the network file server and directory where you want to store student data. Click **Browse** to select a location different from the default. After you select a location, click **Next**.

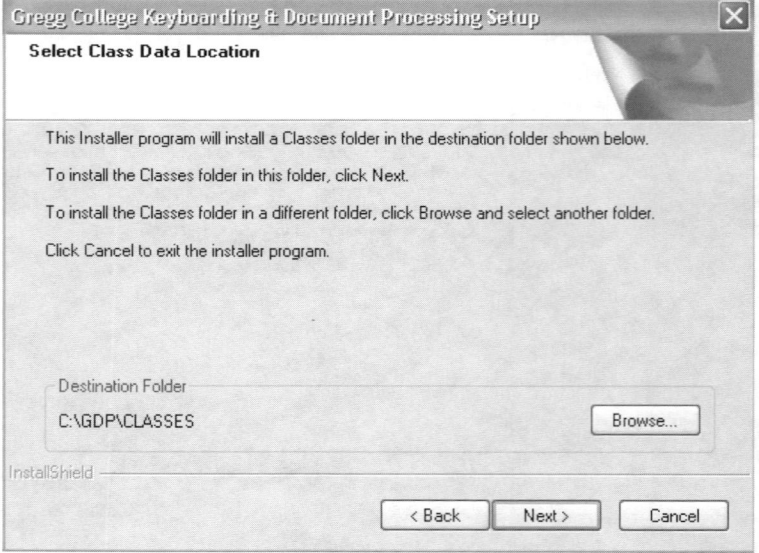

FIGURE 2-4: SELECT CLASS DATA LOCATION DIALOG BOX

9. In the Select Instructors Data Location dialog box (Figure 2-5), locate the network file server and directory where you want to store instructor data (i.e., Gradebook). Click **Browse** to select a location different from the default. After you select a location, click **Next**.

Chapter 2: Installation and Set-Up 9

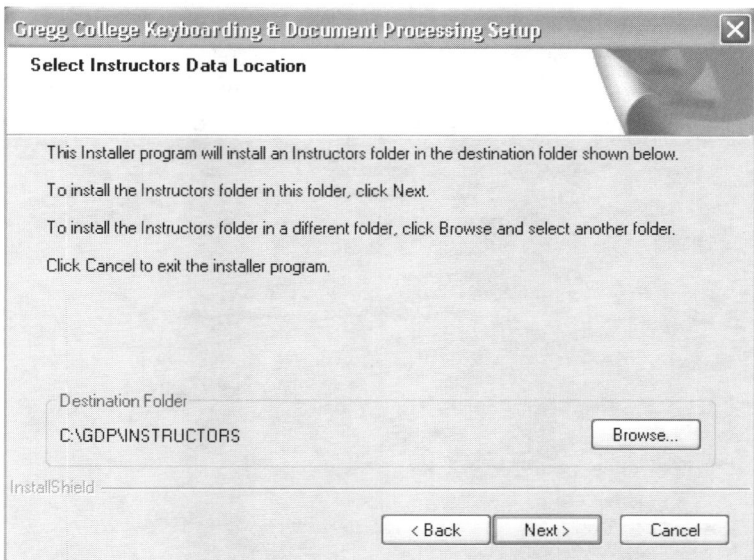

FIGURE 2-5: SELECT INSTRUCTOR'S DATA LOCATION DIALOG BOX

10. The installer copies files to the server and displays the Install Complete dialog box. Click **Finish**.

When you complete the Campus LAN installation, an Irwin Keyboarding program group opens on the desktop and includes this icon, which is used to start GDP:

✦ **Note:** If you installed GDP on the server from a network administrator's workstation rather than from an instructor's workstation, you will have to set up the instructor's workstation to access GDP. The procedure is the same as setting up GDP on student workstations (see "Step 2. Set Up Student and Instructor Access to GDP", next page).

10 Chapter 2: Installation and Set-Up

11. After the GDP installation process is completed, but before exiting the installer, the user will be taken to the electronic registration screen (Figure 2-6). Click **Continue** to go to the product registration screen and fill it out, or click **Cancel** to close the registration screen and exit the installer (Note: Registration is not mandatory. Product registration applies only to the Campus versions of GDP.).

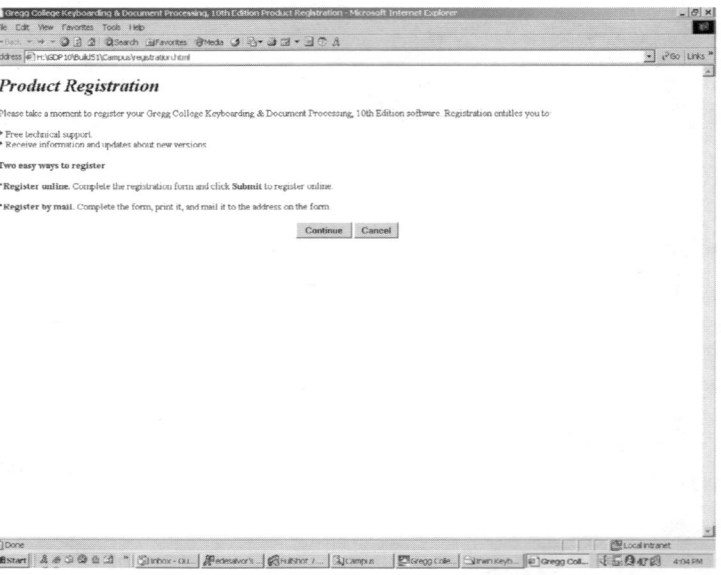

FIGURE 2-6: ELECTRONIC REGISTRATION

2.2.2 Set Up Student and Instructor Access to GDP

After you have installed GDP on the server, follow this procedure for each workstation that will access GDP:

1. Make sure that the student (or instructor) has all rights except supervisory and access control to the following:

   • The student's subdirectory in the CLASSES directory on the network, if you want students to store their work on the network or if you want data to be stored elsewhere but automatically copied to the gradebook on the network,

   • The Microsoft Word directory, if students will be accessing Microsoft Word from the network.

✦ **Note:** Check with your network administrator to determine how to verify or grant access rights on your network.

2. Run the workstation setup program to create an Irwin Keyboarding program group and add a shortcut to the Start menu.

   a. Open the Start menu and choose *Run. . .*

   b. Click **Browse** and locate the network directory where you installed GDP.

   c. Select *Setup.exe* and click **Open** to return to the Run dialog box.

   d. Click **OK** to launch the setup program.

   e. At the Welcome dialog box, click **Next**. At this point, Irwin Keyboarding is added to the Start menu on the workstation. At the Complete dialog box, click **Finish** to exit the program.

✦ **Note:** The Setup program does not create a shortcut to GD10 Instructor Management (LAN) executable in your program group. You can create your own shortcut by locating the GD10IM.EXE file in the installation directory and following the procedures for creating shortcuts, in your Windows User's Guide.

Chapter 2: Installation and Set-Up   **11**

**2.2.3
Add New
Instructor
and Set Up
Classes in
Instructor
Management**

You must first add yourself as a new instructor and then set up your GDP classes before any students use GDP. Here is the procedure:

1. Start GDP and access Instructor Options:

    a. Open the Start menu and choose *Programs*.

    b. Point to *Irwin Keyboarding* and select *GDP Classes*.

    c. The title screen appears, followed by a message telling you that you need to create a class. Click **OK** to close the message dialog box.

    d. Select *Instructor Options* on the Options drop-down menu.

    e. An empty instructor list dialog box opens up (Figure 2-7). Click on **New Instructor** to add yourself as a GDP instructor.

FIGURE 2-7: NEW INSTRUCTOR DIALOG BOX

    f. In the Instructor Options Password dialog box, type **irwin!** And click **OK**.

12   Chapter 2: Installation and Set-Up

g. The Add New Instructor dialog box now displays (Figure 2-8). Fill in the instructor's name, e-mail address and new password (to change it from **irwin!** to a unique password), and then click **Save**.

FIGURE 2-8: ADD NEW INSTRUCTOR DIALOG BOX

h. Select your instructor and click **OK**; then type in the instructor's password and click **OK**. The *Instructor Options with Instructor Management Program* title screen now displays.

 ALERT: Keep the **irwin!** password confidential. It overrides the security provided by the software and gives access to options only the instructor should control. To better ensure security in the future, it is a good idea to change this password for future use. To do so, click on **Change Password** in the Instructor Options Password dialog box.

2. You are now in Instructor Options, which includes the Instructor Management program. Click **LAN Gradebook** in the navigation menu towards the top of the page to open the Classes page (Figure 2-9). (Please note that clicking on **Web Gradebook** will link you to the Instructor Management web site.)

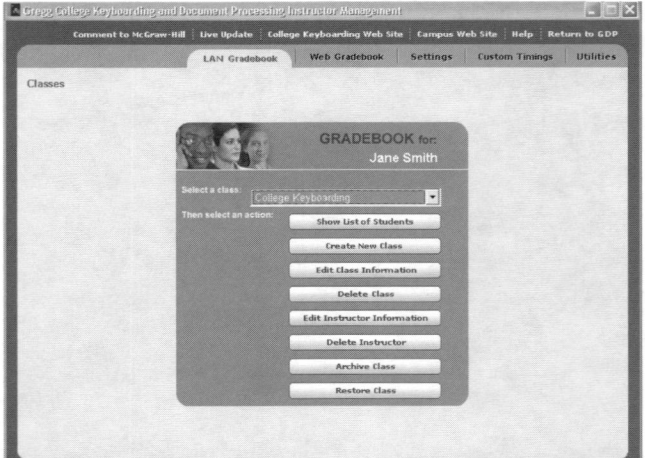

FIGURE 2-9: GRADEBOOK CLASSES PAGE IN THE INSTRUCTOR MANAGEMENT PROGRAM

3. The gradebook is empty, so the only option is to create a new class. Click **Create New Class**.

4. In the Create New Class dialog box (Figure 2-10), complete the required information for the class you want to create.

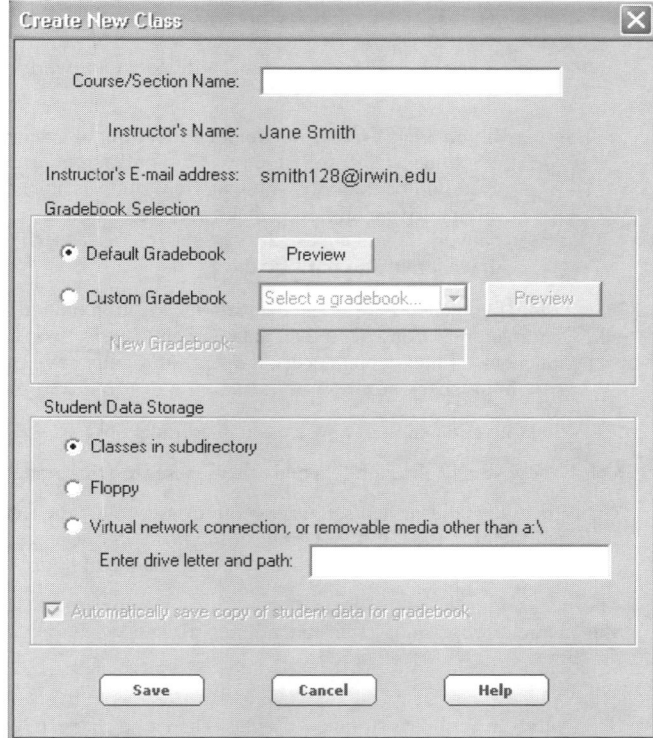

FIGURE 2-10: CREATE NEW CLASS DIALOG BOX

    a. Type a unique identifier for the class (for example, the name of the course and section and day or time of the class) in the **Course/Section Name** field.

    b. The instructor's name and e-mail address fields will be pre-filled with the name and e-mail address for the instructor currently logged on.

    c. Select the type of gradebook to be used – Default Gradebook (the default) or Custom Gradebook. For Default Gradebook, GDP selects the exercises to be graded and automatically enters the grades into the gradebook for those that apply. Click **Preview** next to Default Gradebook to display the default grade scale and a list of the default grading categories and weights.

    d. To use an existing custom gradebook or create a new one, select Custom Gradebook. The "Select a gradebook…" drop-down list includes all of your previously created gradebooks and an option to create a new custom gradebook (i.e., New Gradebook). Once you've created a new custom gradebook with set grading parameters, click **Preview** to display the grade scale and grading categories and weights. Note: A new custom gradebook has no default grade scale, set categories or weights. The grading parameters are determined and set by the instructor.

14   Chapter 2: Installation and Set-Up

   e. In the Student Data Storage area, designate where students in this class will store their work:

   - If you click **Classes in Subdirectory** (the default), each student's data files are stored in the CLASSES subdirectory in the network location specified for Class Data Location when GDP was installed on the server.

   - If you click **Floppy**, students will store their work on a floppy disk in drive A.

   - If you click **Virtual network connection, or removable media other than a:**, students will store their work in a different location, which you must specify. For example, you may have students store their work on Zip disks, thumb drives, on floppy disks in drive B, or in a "virtual" location on a network. If you choose this option, you must specify a location in the **Enter drive letter and path** field.

✦ **Note:** If you choose a student data storage location other than Classes in Subdirectory, a copy of student data will also be saved on the network for the gradebook—unless you uncheck the **Automatically save copy of student data for gradebook** check box.

5. Click **Save** to add your new class to the gradebook.

6. Follow steps 3 through 5 to add other classes to your gradebook.

7. When you are finished setting up your classes, click the **Return to GDP** button on the toolbar in the top right corner of the Instructor Management screen. A dialog box asks if you want to exit Instructor Management and return to GDP. Click **Yes**.

After you set up classes, you can register students into classes using the Instructor Management program or have students self-register when they log on to the GDP for the first time.

✦ **Note:** Student data storage for a class cannot be changed once the first student is registered into the class.

For more detailed information about student registration and data storage options, go to the College Keyboarding Web site at www.mhhe.gdp.com and click on the Technical Tip link.

2.2.4 Specify Instructor and Class Settings

Gregg College Keyboarding & Document Processing™ 10th Edition gives you control over a number of settings so you can customize the way students use GDP. Before your students use GDP for the first time, you should view instructor and class settings and make changes to meet your needs. To do so:

1. Start GDP and access Instructor Options:

   a. Open the Start menu and choose Programs.

   b. Point to the *Irwin Keyboarding* and select *GDP Classes*.

   c. The title screen displays. Select *Instructor Options* on the Options drop-down menu.

   d. In the Instructor Options Password dialog box, type **irwin!** (or your personalized Instructor Options password, if you changed the generic password) and click **OK**.

Chapter 2: Installation and Set-Up   **15**

 ALERT: Keep the Instructor Options password confidential! It overrides the security provided by the software and gives access to options only the instructor should control.

2. Click **Settings** in the navigation menu near the top of the Instructor Options title page. The Settings dialog box (Figure 2-11) displays.

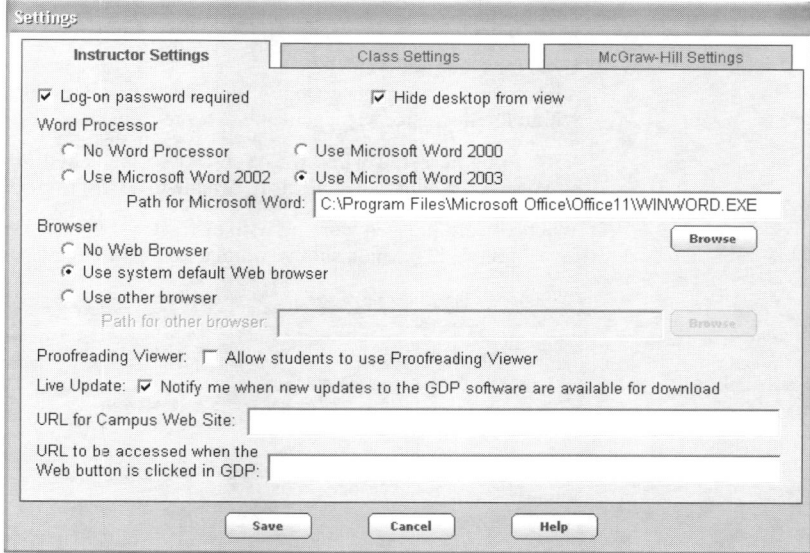

FIGURE 2-11: INSTRUCTOR SETTINGS IN THE SETTINGS DIALOG BOX

3. The Instructor Settings tab appears on top, showing password, hide desktop from view, word processor, browser, proofreading viewer, Live Update, and URL settings for all students using GDP. Review the instructor settings and make any necessary changes.

    Log-on password required   If this box is checked (the default), students will be required to enter their password each time they log on to GDP. If not checked, students will not enter a password when logging on to GDP.

    Hide desktop from view   If this box is checked (the default), the **Hide desktop from view** feature will block out the desktop behind the GDP window, while still providing access to the Start menu and task bar. Instructors must deselect this feature in order to turn it 'off'.

    Word Processor   If **No Word Processor** is selected, students will not be able to do word processing exercises in GDP. If your students have access to Microsoft Word and you want them to be able to work on GDP's word processing exercises, select the correct version of Word and specify the full path. If you do not know the full path to Word, click **Browse** to find it.

    Browser   If **Use system default Web browser** is selected (the default), GDP will launch the default Web browser on the student's system when the student accesses the campus Web site. If **No Web Browser** is selected, students will not be able to access your campus Web site from GDP. If you want your students to be able to access your campus Web site from a browser other than the system default, select **Use other browser** and specify the path to that browser. If you do not know the full path, click **Browse** to find it.

Proofreading Viewer   If this box is checked (this is **not** the default; the instructor must select it to turn it 'on'), students will be able to view their scored text while editing a document so they can see where their errors occurred.

Live Update   If this box is checked (the default), the instructor will be notified when new GDP software updates are available for download. After the instructor logs on, if there is a new update available for download, the Live Update dialog box will display. If this feature is deselected, the instructor will not receive Live Update messages.

URL for Campus Web site   Enter the URL for your school's Web site. If you do not enter a URL for your school's Web site, you will not be able to access it from within the Instructor Management LAN program.

URL to be accessed when the Web button is clicked in GDP   If you have a Web site that you would like students to be able to access from GDP, enter its URL here.

4. When you are finished working with instructor settings, click the Class Settings tab (Figure 2-12), which shows settings for a particular class.

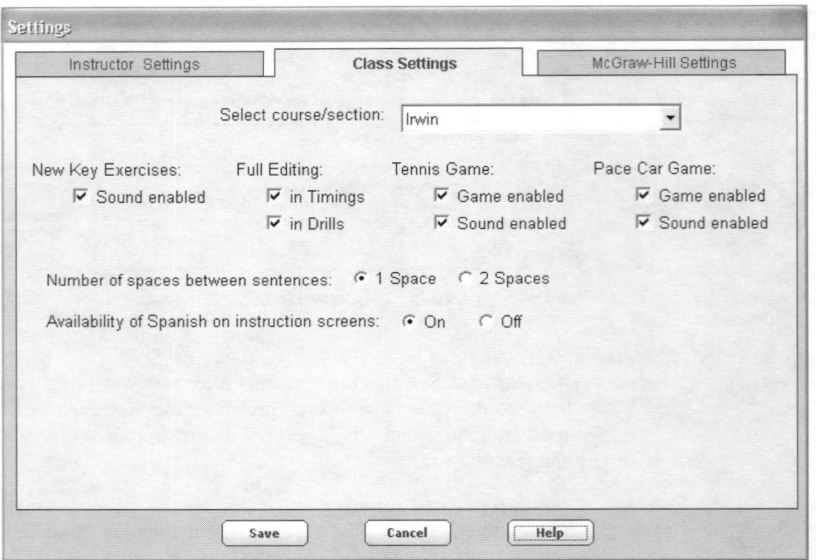

FIGURE 2-12: CLASS SETTINGS IN THE SETTINGS DIALOG BOX

5. Review the class settings and make any necessary changes.

Select Course/Section   This setting shows the currently selected class. Use this list box to view settings for a different class.

New Key Exercises: Sound Enabled   If this box is checked (the default), audio passages will play during new key demonstrations. If unchecked, new key demonstrations will not include audio passages.

Full Editing: in Timings   If this box is checked (the default), students will be able to edit text in timed writings. If unchecked, editing will be disabled during timed writings.

Chapter 2: Installation and Set-Up 17

Full Editing: in Drills   If this box is checked (the default), students will be able to edit text in drills. If unchecked, editing will be disabled during drills.

Tennis Game: Game enabled   If this box is checked (the default), students will be able to play the tennis game, which is accessible from the Games menu. If unchecked, the tennis game will be inactive.

Tennis Game: Sound enabled   If this box is checked (the default), there will be sound accompanying the tennis game. (Sound can also be disabled from the Game Options screen.)

Pace Car Game: Game enabled   If this box is checked (the default), students will be able to play the pace car game, which is accessible from the Games menu. If unchecked, the pace car game will be inactive.

Pace Car Game: Sound enabled   If this box is checked (the default), there will be sound accompanying the pace car game.

Number of spaces between sentences   Click on the appropriate radio button to identify whether students in a class will use one space or two spaces following punctuation at the end of a sentence (the default is **1 Space**).

Availability of Spanish on instruction screens   Click on the appropriate radio button to either enable or disable the Spanish translation capability on instruction screens. The default is "**On**"; if the instructor chooses to turn this feature "**Off**", the **English** and **Espanol** buttons will be removed from the screen.

✦   **Note:** Consistent with the *Gregg College Keyboarding & Document Processing*™ *10th Edition* textbook, the GDP software uses one space (the default setting) after all punctuation marks (periods, colons, etc.).

6. When you are finished working with the settings, click **Save** to record your changes and close the Settings dialog box.

ALERT: Do not change any information in the McGraw-Hill Settings tab unless specifically instructed to do so by McGraw-Hill.

2.2.5 Register Students into GDP Classes

Once you have completed the installation and set-up, students can register themselves into classes and begin working in GDP. For detailed instructions, see 3.1 Logging On on page 33.

If you prefer, you can pre-register students into classes using Instructor Management. For more information, see "Adding a Student to a Class" in Chapter 5 (Instructor Management LAN) or Chapter 6 (Instructor Management Web site) of the User's Guide.

✦   **Note:** Campus-based students who have already used GDP with floppy disks cannot self-register. See Chapter 5 of the GDP User's Guide for information on adding students with floppy disks with which they have already logged on.

✦ **Note:** The Campus with Instructor Management (LAN) configuration includes the option of Distance-Learning for students (i.e., either a system that has MAPI-compliant e-mail enabled or uses a student upload Web site to move data to the Instructor Management Web site). Please further note that an instructor must have his or her class set up in the Instructor Management Web site in order for the Distance Learning feature to work.

If you want to install GDP so that you can upload student data to the Instructor Management Web site, verify that the system has MAPI-compliant e-mail enabled (such as Microsoft Outlook or Outlook Express).

MAPI, an acronym for Messaging Application Program Interface, enables a Windows application to send e-mail. The MAPI standard provides many benefits, such as the ability to save mail in an "Outbox" for sending later when you are connected to the Internet. The MAPI standard was created by Microsoft and is supported by a number of third-party vendors, including Eudora and Netscape. Microsoft includes MAPI support in e-mail programs such as Outlook Express and Outlook. Many Internet Service Providers (ISPs) provide a MAPI-compliant e-mail program as part of their installed software since they include Microsoft Outlook Express® as the e-mail program. Properly configuring a system for sending e-mail using MAPI requires information from the ISP, such as the address of the ISP's mail server. For this reason, it is not possible to give general instructions for configuring e-mail on any workstation.

For additional tips on using the distance learning capabilities of the GDP software please visit the following Web site: www.mhhe.gdp.com

Chapter 2: Installation and Set-Up   19

2.3 Campus without Instructor Management (Standalone) Installation and Set-Up

The Campus without Instructor Management (Standalone) version of GDP is covered here; this configuration denotes that students will either provide instructors with their work manually or upload it to the Instructor Management Web site, using the distance-learning option.

2.3.1 Install GDP without Instructor Management on a Standalone Workstation

1. Turn on the workstation and start Windows.

2. Put the GDP CD-ROM in your CD-ROM drive.

3. No auto-run.

   a. Open the Start menu (on the Windows task bar) and choose *Run. . .*

   b. In the Open blank, type **d:\setup** (please note that the CD-ROM drive could be **e:** on some computers). Click **OK**.

4. The InstallShield Wizard loads, then the Welcome dialog box displays. Click **Next** to continue.

5. In the License Agreement dialog box (Figure 2-13), click **I accept**… to accept the terms of the license agreement. Click **Next** to continue. Note: you must accept the license agreement to continue with the installation process.

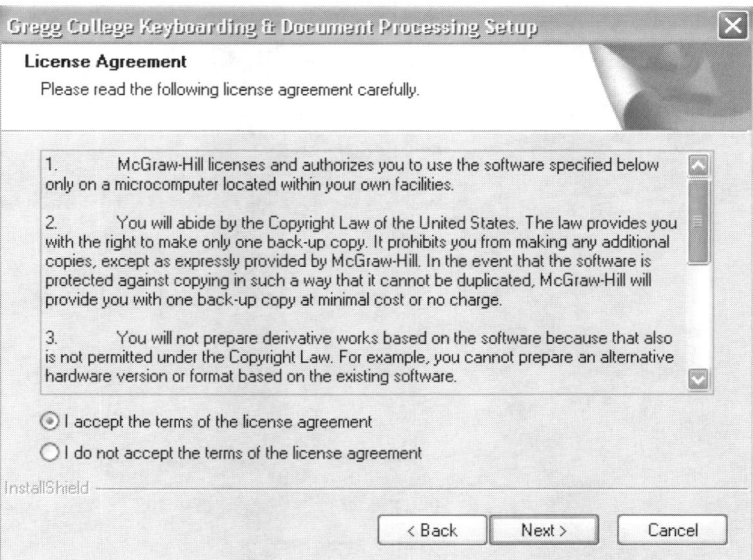

FIGURE 2-13: SELECT LICENSE AGREEMENT DIALOG BOX

6. In the Select Components (Figure 2-14) dialog box, click **No** to indicate that you are installing GDP without Instructor Management. Then click **Next** to continue.

20 Chapter 2: Installation and Set-Up

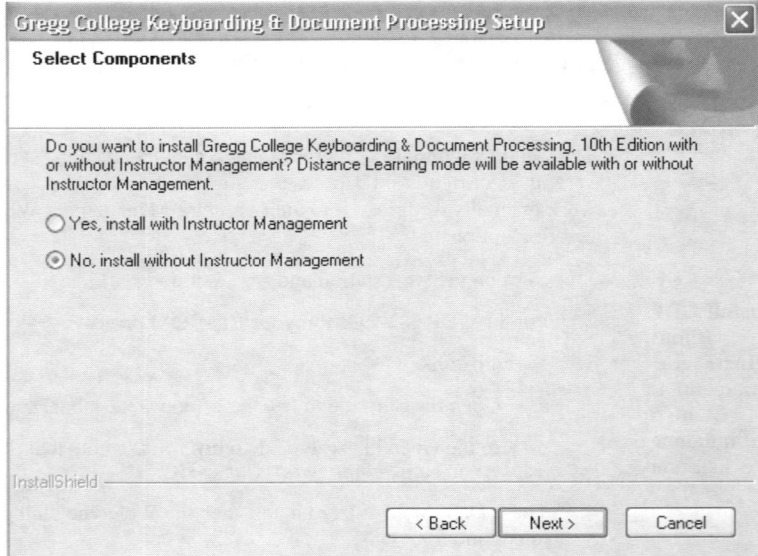

FIGURE 2-14: SELECT COMPONENTS DIALOG

7. In the Select Destination Location dialog box (Figure 2-15), choose the local hard-disk location where you want to install the GDP software. Click **Browse** to select a location different from the default. After you select a location, click **Next**.

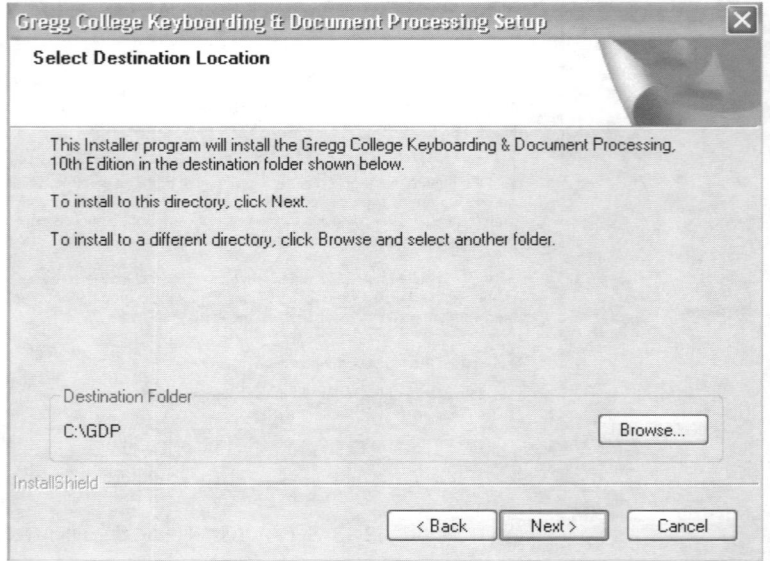

FIGURE 2-15: SELECT DESTINATION LOCATION DIALOG BOX

Chapter 2: Installation and Set-Up 21

8. In the Select Student Data Location dialog box (Figure 2-16), choose an option and click **Next**.

- Select **Save student data on C:\ or other media** (the default) if the student will store work in a data directory on the local hard drive or on other removable media such as a Zip disk. If you choose this option, the Select Student Data Path dialog box will open once you click the **Next** button.

- Select **Save student data on floppy disk A:** if the student will store work on a floppy disk in drive A.

- Select **Save student data on floppy disk B:** if the student will store work on a floppy disk in drive B.

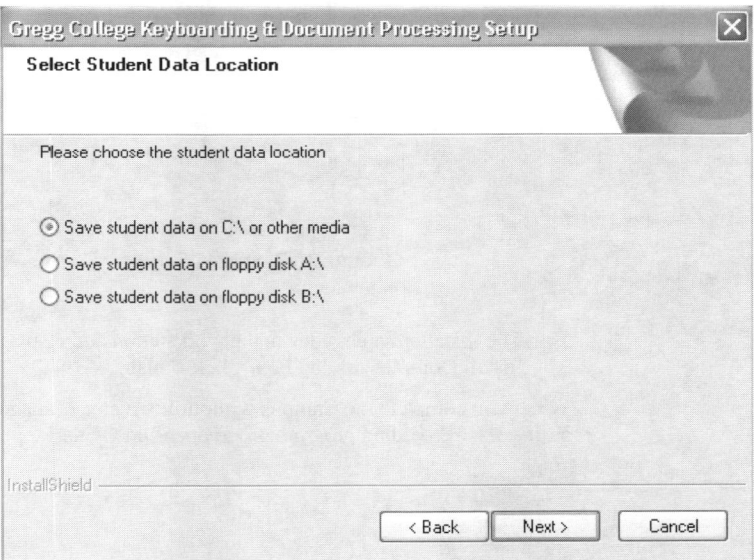

FIGURE 2-16: SELECT STUDENT DATA LOCATION DIALOG BOX

9. In the Select Student Data Path dialog box (Figure 2-17), you specify the location where student data will be stored (if you chose to save student data on C:\ or other media in the previous dialog box). Click **Next** to accept the default destination folder (C:\GDPDATA), or click **Browse** to select a different location and then click **Next**.

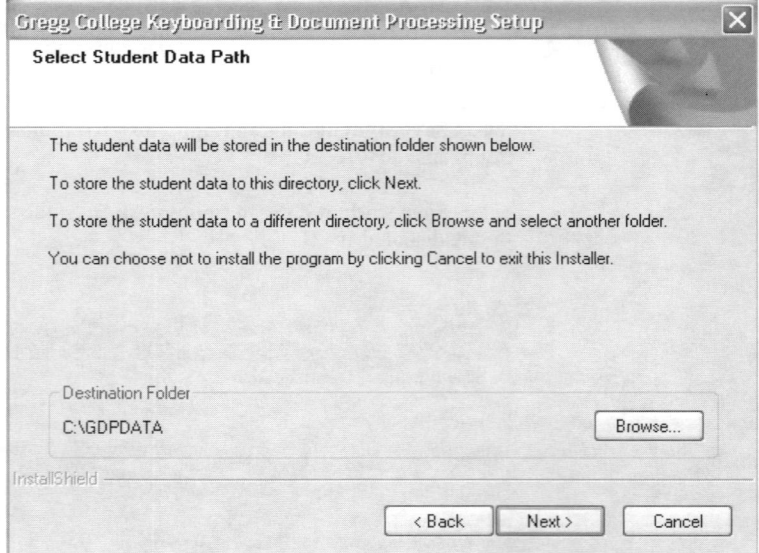

FIGURE 2-17: SELECT STUDENT DATA PATH DIALOG BOX

10. The installer copies files to the workstation and displays the Install Complete dialog box. Click **Finish**.

When you complete the Campus without Instructor Management (standalone) installation, an Irwin Keyboarding program group opens on the desktop with this icon for starting GDP:

2.3.2 Specify Settings for the Campus without Instructor Management Configuration

Gregg College Keyboarding & Document Processing™ 10th Edition gives you control over a number of settings so you can customize the way students use GDP. Before students use GDP for the first time, you should view instructor and class settings and make changes to meet your needs. To do so:

1. Start GDP and access Instructor Options:

   a. Open the Start menu and choose *Programs*.

   b. Point to *Irwin Keyboarding* and select *GDP Standalone*.

   c. The title screen displays. Select *Instructor Options* on the Options drop-down menu.

   d. In the Instructor Options Password dialog box, type **irwin!** and click **OK**.

Chapter 2: Installation and Set-Up **23**

 ALERT: Keep the **irwin!** password confidential. It overrides the security provided by the software and gives access to options only the instructor should control. To better ensure security in the future, it is a good idea to change this password for future use. To do so, click on **Change Password** in the Instructor Options Password dialog box.

2. Click **Settings** in the navigation menu towards the top of the Instructor Options title page. The Settings dialog box (Figure 2-18) displays.

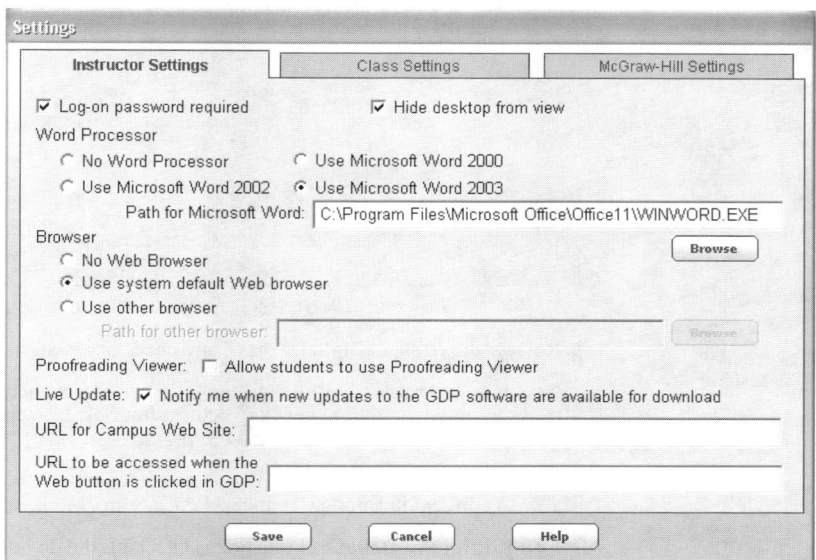

FIGURE 2-18: INSTRUCTOR SETTINGS IN THE SETTINGS DIALOG

3. The Instructor Settings tab appears on top, showing password, hide desktop from view, word processor, browser, proofreading viewer, Live Update, and URL settings for all students using GDP. Review the instructor settings and make any necessary changes. The instructor settings in the Campus without Instructor Management (standalone) configuration are the same as those for the Campus with Instructor Management (LAN) version. For specific information on instructor settings, see 2.2.4 Specify Instructor and Class Settings, starting on page 14.

4. When you are finished working with instructor settings, click the Class Settings tab (Figure 2-19), which shows the various settings for GDP exercises.

24   Chapter 2: Installation and Set-Up

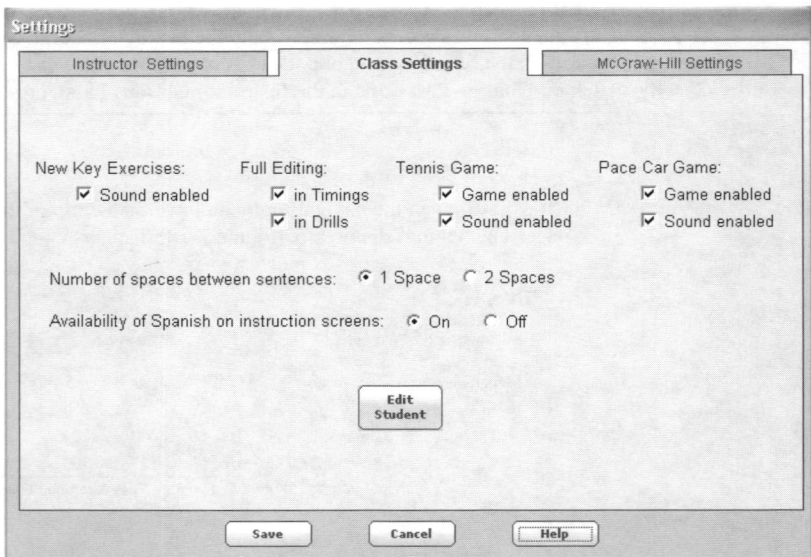

FIGURE 2-19: CLASS SETTINGS IN THE SETTINGS DIALOG BOX

5. Review the class settings and make any necessary changes.

New Key Exercises: Sound enabled   If this box is checked (the default), audio passages will play during new key demonstrations. If unchecked, new key demonstrations will not include audio passages.

Full Editing: in Timings   If this box is checked (the default), students will be able to edit text in timings. If unchecked, editing will be disabled during timings.

Full Editing: in Drills   If this box is checked (the default), students will be able to edit text in drills. If unchecked, editing will be disabled during drills.

Tennis Game: Game enabled   If this box is checked (the default), students will be able to play the tennis game, which is accessible from the Games menu. If unchecked, the tennis game will be inactive.

Tennis Game: Sound enabled   If this box is checked (the default), there will be sound accompanying the tennis game. (Sound can also be disabled from the Game Options screen.)

Pace Car Game: Game enabled   If this box is checked (the default), students will be able to play the pace car game, which is accessible from the Games menu. If unchecked, the pace car game will be inactive.

Pace Car Game: Sound enabled   If this box is checked (the default), there will be sound accompanying the pace car game.

Number of spaces between sentences   Click on the appropriate radio button to identify whether students in a class will use one space or two spaces following punctuation at the end of a sentence (the default is **1 Space**).

Availability of Spanish on instruction screens   Click on the appropriate radio button to either enable or disable the Spanish translation capability on instruction screens. The default is "**On**"; if the instructor chooses to turn this feature "**Off**", the **English** and **Espanol** buttons will be removed from the screen.

Chapter 2: Installation and Set-Up   **25**

6. When you are finished working with the settings, click **Save** to record your changes and close the Settings dialog box.

Note: The Campus without Instructor Management (Standalone) configuration includes the option of Distance-Learning for students (i.e., either a system that has MAPI-compliant e-mail enabled or uses a student upload Web site to move data to the Instructor Management Web site). Please further note that an instructor must have his or her class set up in the Instructor Management Web site in order for the Distance-Learning feature to work.

ALERT: Do not change any information in the McGraw-Hill Settings tab unless specifically instructed to do so by McGraw-Hill.

2.4 Set Up the Instructor Management Web Site for Distance Learners

Please follow this procedure to register an instructor and set up his or her classes in the Instructor Management Web site, so that students can use GDP's Distance-Learning feature (Note: The **Web Gradebook** button that allows access to the Instructor Management Web site is only available via the two Campus configurations (with Instructor Management and without Instructor Management), and not the Home configuration.).

2.4 Set Up the Instructor Management Web site for Distance Learners

1. Start GDP and access Instructor Options:

   a. Open the Start menu and choose *Programs*.

   b. Point to *Irwin Keyboarding* and select either *GDP Classes* or *GDP Standalone*.

   c. The title screen displays. Select *Instructor Options* on the Options drop-down menu. If you are using GDP with Instructor Management, select your name from the instructor list and click **OK**.

   d. In the appropriate Password dialog box, type **irwin!** (or your personalized Instructor Options password, if you changed the generic password) and click **OK**.

ALERT: Keep the Instructor Options password confidential! It overrides the security provided by the software and gives access to options only the instructor should control.

2. Click **Web Gradebook** in the navigation menu towards the top of the Instructor Options title page. When you do this, your browser launches the Instructor Management Web site and goes to the log-on page.

3. The first time you log on to the Instructor Management Web site, you will need to register and log on as a new user:

   a. On the log-on page, type your e-mail address in the **Your e-mail address** field and **irwin!** in the **Your password** field. Then click **Log-on**.

   b. The Instructor Registration page displays next. Verify your e-mail address and enter your school information, along with your first and last names in the fields provided. Then click **Register**. When you do this, the Web site sends your personal password to your e-mail address within a few minutes and returns you to the log-on page. You will need your personal password to enter the Instructor Management Web site.

   c. Once you receive the e-mail with your personal password, you are registered with the site. On the log-on page, re-enter your e-mail address, type your new personal password, and click **Log-on**. (You can change your personal password at any time by clicking **Change Password** on the log-on page.)

Your registration information is now complete. Subsequently, when you log on to the Instructor Management Web site, you will simply type your e-mail address and personal password and go directly to the Gradebook page.

Chapter 2: Installation and Set-Up   27

4. Your next step is to add classes to the Instructor Management Web site:

   a. On the Gradebook page, click **Create New Class**.

   b. On the Create a New Class page, type a unique identifier for the class (for example, the name of the course and the section and day or time of the class) in the **Course/Section Name** field. Then select the "Gregg College Keyboarding and Document Processing, 10th Edition" radio button under software used in class. Select the checkbox "Notify me when student uploads new work", if you want to be notified by e-mail. Then click **Save** to return to the Gradebook page with your new class added.

   c. Repeat steps a and b to add other classes to your gradebook.

5. Students register themselves to use GDP the first time they log on. (For more information, see 3.1 Logging On on page 33.) However, you must add students to your classes on the Instructor Management Web site before students can upload their data to the Web site. To add a student to a class:

   a. Select the class on the Gradebook page and click **Show List of Students**.

   b. On the List of Students page, click **Add New Student**.

   c. On the Add New Student page, enter the student's e-mail address and click **Save**. When you first add students' e-mail addresses, only their e-mail addresses will appear in the Gradebook. Once students register and upload data to the Instructor Management Web site, the Gradebook will be updated so that the student's name is displayed along with his or her e-mail address.

 For detailed information about issues related to student e-mail addresses, go to the College Keyboarding Web site at www.mhhe.gdp.com and click the Technical Tips link.

6. Distance-learning students upload their data to the Instructor Management Web site so you can view their work. For detailed information, see 3.7.1 Sending Distance-Learning Student Data to the Instructor Management Web site on page 45.

2.5 Home Installation and Set-Up

To install the Home version of GDP, please use the following procedure:

2.5.1 Install GDP on the Home Computer

1. Turn on the computer and start Windows.
2. Put the GDP CD-ROM in the CD-ROM drive.
3. No auto-run.
   a. Open the Start menu (on the Windows task bar) and choose *Run. . .*
   b. In the Open blank, type **d:\setup** (please note that the CD-ROM drive could be **e:** on some computers). Click **OK**.
   c. The InstallShield Wizard loads, then the Welcome dialog box displays. Click **Next** to continue.
4. In the License Agreement dialog box (Figure 2-20), click **I accept**… to accept the terms of the license agreement. Click **Next** to continue. Note: You must accept the license agreement to continue with the installation process.

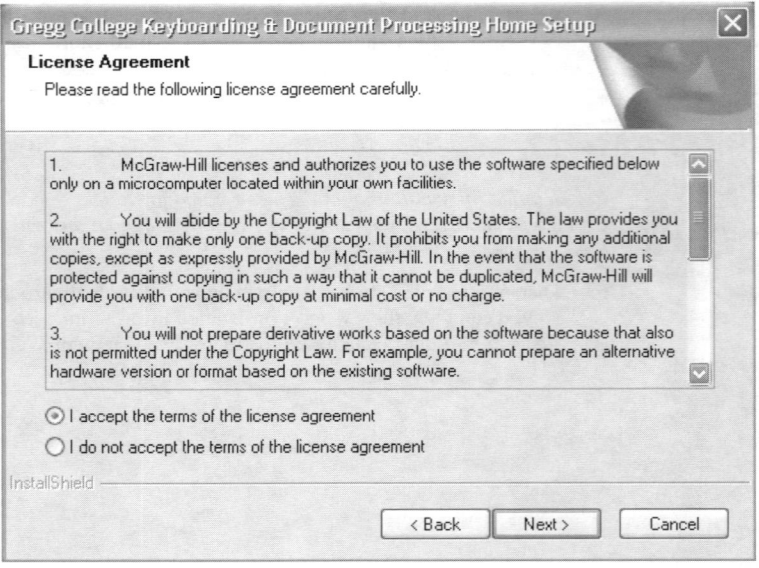

FIGURE 2-20: LICENSE AGREEMENT DIALOG BOX

Chapter 2: Installation and Set-Up   29

5. In the Select Destination Location dialog box (Figure 2-21), choose the local hard-disk location where you want to install the GDP software. Click **Browse** to select a location different from the default. After you select a location, click **Next**.

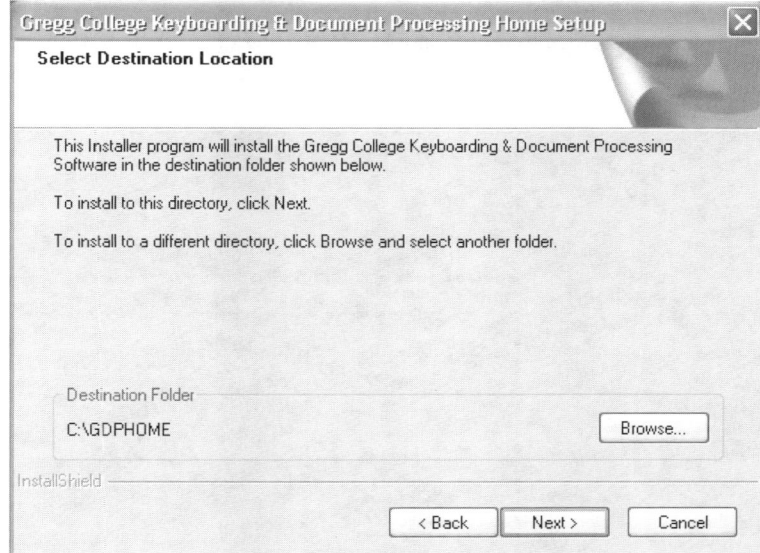

FIGURE 2-21: SELECT DESTINATION LOCATION DIALOG BOX

6. In the Select Student Data Location dialog box (Figure 2-22), choose an option and click **Next**.

- Select **Save student data on other media** (the default) to store student work in a data directory on the local hard disk or on other removable media such as a Zip disk. If you choose this option, the Select Student Data Path dialog box will open once you click the Next button.

- Select **Save student data on floppy disk A:** if the student will store work on a floppy disk in drive A.

- Select **Save student data on floppy disk B:** if the student will store work on a floppy disk in drive B.

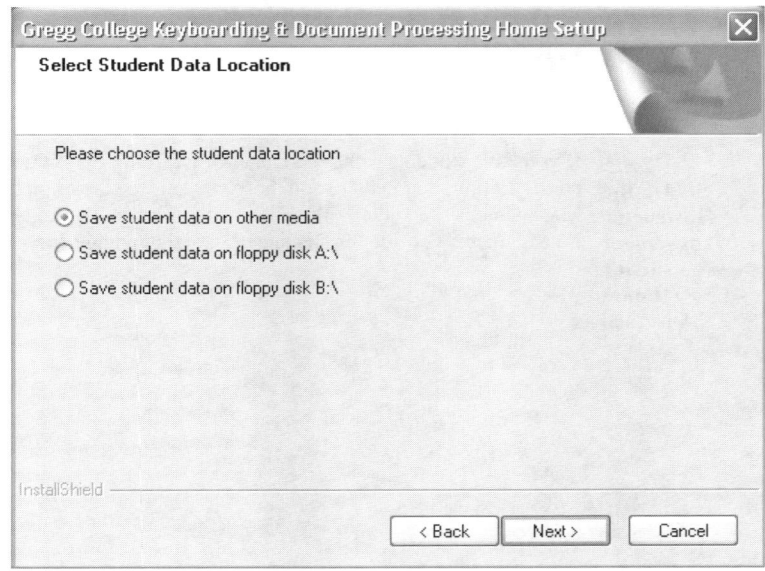

FIGURE 2-22: SELECT STUDENT DATA LOCATION DIALOG BOX

7. In the Select Student Data Path dialog box (Figure 2-23), you specify the location where student data will be stored (if you chose to save student data on other media in the previous dialog box). Click **Next** to accept the default destination folder (C:\GDPDATA), or click **Browse** to select a different location and then click **Next**.

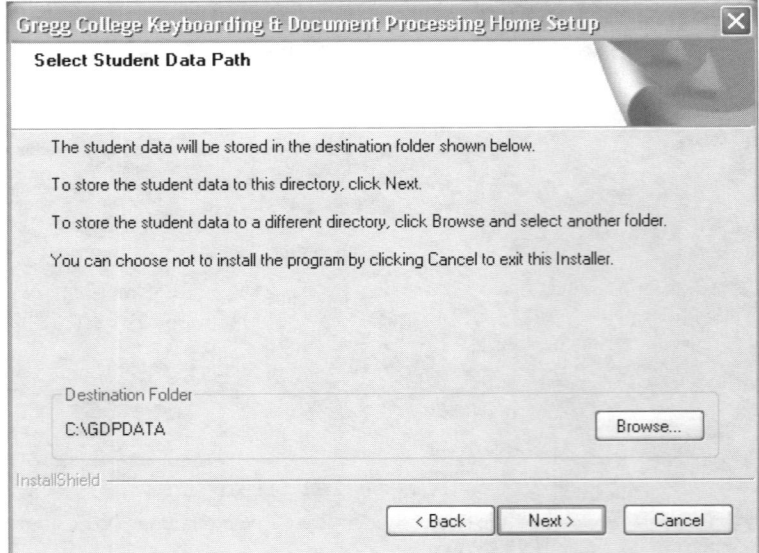

FIGURE 2-23: SELECT STUDENT DATA PATH DIALOG BOX

8. The installer copies files for the workstation and displays the Install Complete dialog box. Click **Finish**.

When you complete the Home installation, an Irwin Keyboarding program group opens on the desktop and the following icon for starting GDP:

2.5.2 Set Up the Instructor Management Web site for (Home) Distance Learners

If you have students using the Distance-Learning option within the GDP Home configuration, you need to add those students to classes on the Instructor Management Web site. Follow the instructions in 2.4 Set Up the Instructor Management Web site for Distance Learners on page 26.

2.6 About Student Data Files

Students' work in GDP can be stored on floppy disks or other removable media, on a local hard-disk drive, or on a network drive. If you want to store student data files on a local or network hard-disk drive, you will need approximately 5 MB of disk space per student.

You specify the location of student data files at the end of the GDP installation procedure (if you are setting up a Campus without Instructor Management or Home configuration) or when you set up GDP classes (if you are setting up a Campus with Instructor Management (LAN) configuration).

2.6.1 Getting Student Data into Instructor Management

The process of loading student data into Instructor Management varies according to the configuration.

- In a Campus with Instructor Management (LAN) configuration, student data is automatically loaded in the Instructor Management program on the LAN so you can compute grades and track student progress with no additional work. (If students are not storing their work on the network, make sure that the "Automatically save a copy of student data for gradebook" box is checked for the class in the gradebook.)

- In the two standalone configurations—without Instructor Management and Home—you must collect student data files and manually load them into the Instructor Management program on an instructor workstation before you can compute grades and track student progress.

- When using the Distance-Learning option in any of the GDP configurations, students use the Upload button to upload their data from their hard drive or a data disk to the Instructor Management Web site, where you can compute grades and track student progress. The student's data is sent in an e-mail to the Instructor Management Web site within a half hour to two hours.

2.6.2 Changing the Student Data Location

The ability to change the student data location also varies according to the configuration.

- If you are using the Instructor Management program in the Campus with Instructor Management (LAN) configuration, you can change the student data location for a class if no students are registered in the class. As soon as the first student registers into a class, the student data location cannot be changed. If it is necessary to change the location for a class with registered students, create a new class with the desired data location, and then transfer students from the original class into the new class. Delete the old class after all students have been transferred to the new class.

- If you are not using the Instructor Management program, you can change the student data location at any time. To do so, you need to change the shortcut path for the GDP program icon. For example, if you originally set up a student to store data in a data directory on the hard disk and you want to now store the student's data on a floppy drive A, you would change the shortcut from **C:\GDP\GDP.EXE C:\GDPDATA.** (Where C: is you hard disk, \GDP is the directory where GDP is installed, and \GDPDATA is the directory for storing student data) to **C:\GDP\GDP.EXE A:\.**

For detailed information on changing the location of student data, go to the College Keyboarding Web site at www.mhhe.gdp.com and click on the Technical Tip link.

2.6.3 Backing up Student Data Files

Remember to update and back up student data files regularly.

- If your students use floppy disks to store their work, tell students to make back-up copies of their data disks on a regular basis.

- If you are storing data on a hard-disk drive or are using the Instructor Management program, it is important to make regular back-ups of the GDP data directory and the GDP program directory and all of its subdirectories. Failure to do so could result in data loss or corruption in the event of a power outage or other unforeseen system problems.

Chapter 3: Using GDP

3.1 Logging On

The log-on process varies according to the GDP configuration installed and the extent to which you have set up GDP classes and registered your students into those classes.

3.1.1 Logging on to the Campus with Instructor Management (LAN) Version

Before students can log on to the Campus with Instructor Management (LAN) version of GDP, you must have created a class for them in the Instructor Management program. (For more information, see 2.2 Campus with Instructor Management (LAN) Installation and Set-Up on page 9.) Once you have set up GDP classes for your students, they can log on to student workstations as follows:

1. The student turns on the student workstation and starts windows.

2. From the Start menu (on the Windows task bar), the student chooses *Programs* and points to *Irwin Keyboarding*.

3. The student selects [GDP Classes].

4. The title screen displays for several seconds, followed by the log-on screen (Figure 3-1). To advance to the log-on screen immediately, the student can click anywhere on the title screen.

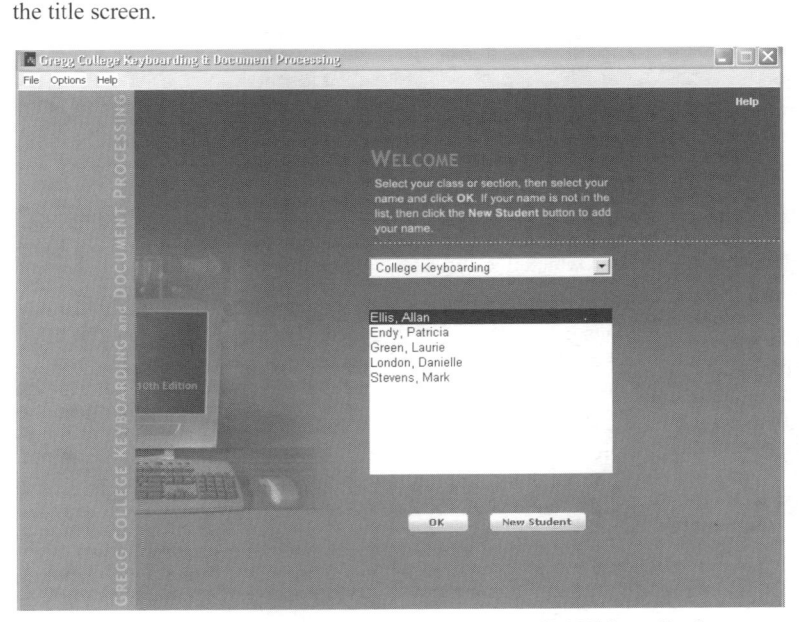

FIGURE 3-1: CAMPUS WITH INSTRUCTOR MANAGEMENT (LAN) LOG-ON SCREEN

5. The student selects the class or section by highlighting its name on the list box.

6. The student list opens for the selected class.

   - If already registered into the class, the student highlights his or her name on the student list and clicks **OK**.

   - If not on the list, the student must register into the class by clicking **New Student**.

7. The student completes the on-screen registration form and clicks **Save**.

8. GDP registers the student's information, and Tutorial pops up in a window on the screen. The Tutorial provides first-time users an overview of how GDP works.

9. If you have posted a class announcement, it appears when the student finishes the Tutorial. To close the window, the student clicks **OK**.

10. To begin working in GDP, the student selects a lesson from the Lessons menu, which displays next. For information about working on GDP exercises, see 3.2 Working on Lesson Exercises on page 37.

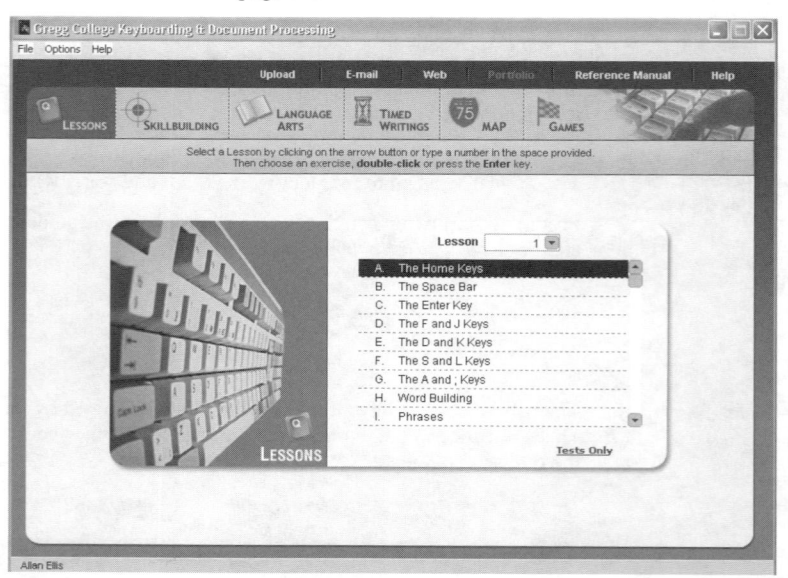

FIGURE 3-2: LESSONS MENU

✦ **Note:** Subsequently when logging on to GDP, the student simply selects his or her class and name and types his or her password. GDP will open the Lessons menu to the lesson upon which the student last worked.

3.1.2
Logging on Initially as a Campus without Instructor Management (Standalone) or Distance-Learning Student

Note: Before distance-learning students can send their data to the Instructor Management Web site, you need to register them at the site. (For more information, see 2.4 Set Up the Instructor Management Web site for Distance Learners on page 26.) Once you have registered your students on the Instructor Management Web site, they can log on to GDP and upload their work to the Instructor Management Web site.

Here is the procedure for a standalone student (the Campus without Instructor Management configuration or a Distance-Learning student using this configuration) logging on to GDP for the first time:

1. The student turns on the computer and starts Windows.

2. If using a floppy disk to store student data, the student puts a floppy disk in the floppy drive.

3. From the Start menu (on the Windows task bar), the student chooses *Programs* and points to *Irwin Keyboarding*.

4. The student selects ![GDP Standalone].

5. The title screen displays for several seconds, followed by the log-on screen (Figure 3-3). (To advance to the log-on screen immediately, the student can click anywhere on the title screen.)

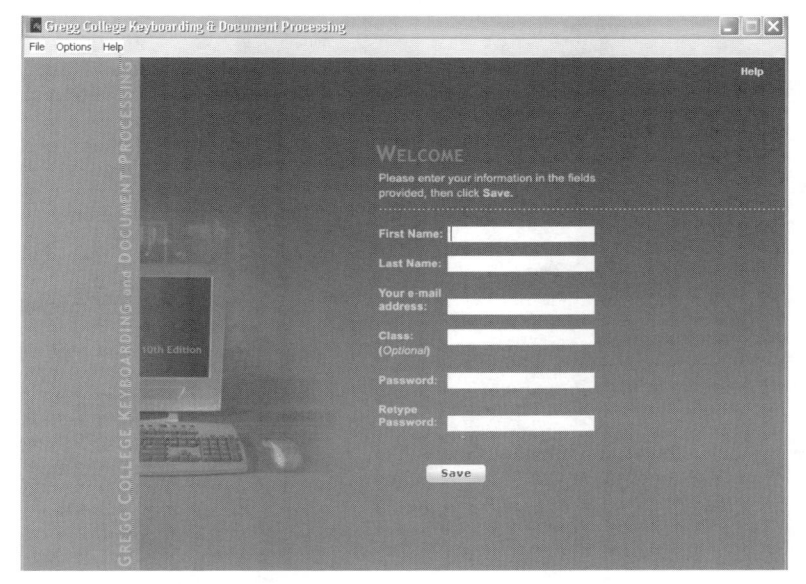

FIGURE 3-3: CAMPUS WITHOUT INSTRUCTOR MANAGEMENT (STANDALONE) LOG-ON SCREEN

6. The student completes the registration information on the log-on screen and clicks **Save**.

7. GDP registers the student's information, and the Tutorial pops up in a window on the screen. The Tutorial provides first-time users an overview of how GDP works.

8. To begin working in GDP, the student selects a lesson from the Lessons menu, which displays next. For information about working on GDP exercises, see "Working on Lesson Exercises" later in this chapter.

✦ **Note:** Subsequently when logging on to GDP, the standalone student simply types his or her password. GDP will open the Lessons menu to the lesson upon which the student last worked.

✦ **Note:** At any time during a GDP session, the distance-learning student can send his or her data to the Instructor Management Web site by clicking the **Upload** button on the toolbar. When the distance- learning student logs off, GDP automatically prompts the student to update his or her data on the Instructor Management Web site if the student's data has changed since the last upload. For more information on uploading data to the Instructor Management Web site, see 3.7.1 Sending Distance-Learning Student Data to the Instructor Management Web Site on page 45.

**3.1.3
Logging on as
a Home
Student**

When accessing the GDP Home version for the first time, the student will be asked to register his or her first and last name ("e-mail address" and "class" are optional) in the appropriate fields and then click **Save**. Subsequently when accessing the GDP Home version, the student will be taken directly to the Lessons Menu (there is no log-on screen in the GDP Home configuration).

If the student selected removable media or a floppy disk drive for data storage in the Home version of GDP (during installation) and doesn't have it inserted when accessing GDP, he or she will be prompted with the following: "Please insert your student data disk and click **OK**. If you have not yet created your student data diskette, then click the **New Student** button."

Unlike the Campus versions of GDP, the Home version's settings are controlled by the student rather than the instructor. The first time the student registers within the Home version of *Gregg College Keyboarding & Document Processing™ 10th Edition*, he or she should check word processing, browser, e-mail, and other settings for using GDP. To do so:

1. After initial registration, the student selects *Settings* on the Options drop-down menu to open the Settings dialog box (Figure 3-4).

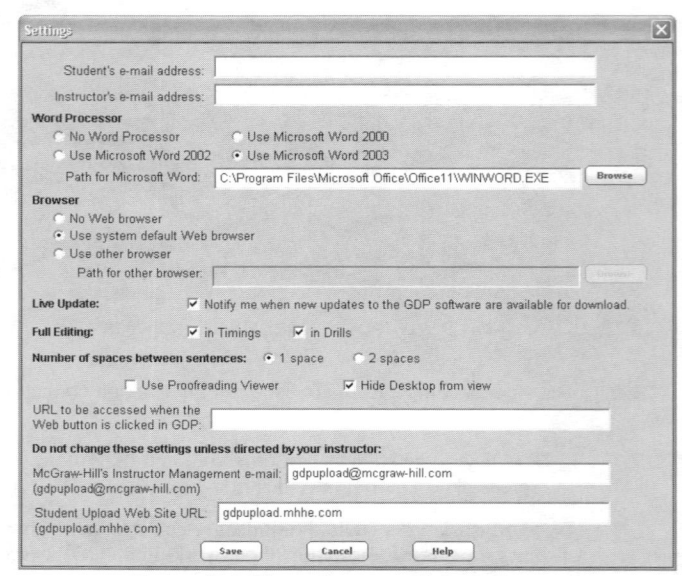

FIGURE 3-4: HOME SETTINGS DIALOG BOX

2. The student reviews the settings and makes any necessary changes.

Student's e-mail address The student's e-mail address can be added here or as part of the student's initial registration information. If the address changes after initial registration, the student must make the change in the Settings dialog box so that data is properly uploaded to the Instructor Management Web site.

Instructor's e-mail address This is the instructor's e-mail address for the class and can be edited.

Word Processor If the student's computer does not have Microsoft Word, **No Word Processor** should be selected. In this case, the student will not be able to do the word processing exercises in GDP. Otherwise, select the correct version of Microsoft Word and specify its full path.

Browser   If **Use System default Web browser** is selected (the default), GDP will launch the system's default Web browser when the student accesses the campus Web site. If **No Web browser** is selected, the student will not be able to access the campus Web site from GDP. If the student wants to access the campus Web site through GDP using a browser other than the system default, **Use other browser** should be selected and the full path to it specified. If you do not know the full path, click **Browse** to find it.

Live Update   If this box is checked (the default), the student will be notified when new GDP software updates are available for download. After the student accesses GDP, if there is a new update available for download, the Live Update dialog box will display. If this feature is deselected, the student will not receive Live Update messages.

Full Editing: in Timings   If this box is checked (the default), the student will be able to edit text in timed writings. If unchecked, editing will be disabled during timed writings.

Full Editing: in Drills   If this box is checked (the default), the student will be able to edit text in drills. If unchecked, editing will be disabled during drills.

Number of spaces between sentences   Click on the appropriate radio button to identify whether the student will use one space or two spaces following punctuation at the end of a sentence (the default is **1 Space**).

Use Proofreading Viewer   If this box is checked (this is **not** the default; the student must select it to turn it 'on'), the student will be able to view his or her scored text while editing a document so he/she can see where his or her errors occurred.

Hide Desktop from view   If this box is checked (the default), the **Hide Desktop from view** feature will block out the desktop behind the GDP window, while still providing access to the Start menu and task bar. The student must deselect this feature in order to turn it 'off'.

URL to be accessed when the Web button is clicked in GDP   If you have a Web site that you would like students to be able to access from GDP, tell students to enter its URL here.

McGraw-Hill's Instructor Management e-mail   The student should not change this setting unless specifically instructed to do so by McGraw-Hill. This is the address where uploaded student data is sent when using the Distance-Learning option.

Student Upload Web Site URL   Again, the student should not change this setting unless specifically instructed to do so by McGraw-Hill. This is the URL used to upload student data when using the Distance-Learning option.

3. When finished working with settings, the student clicks **Save** to record changes and close the Settings dialog box.

3.2 Working on Lesson Exercises

After the student logs on, the Lessons menu (Figure 3-5) displays the list of exercises in the current lesson. If the student is using GDP for the first time, Lesson 1 exercises are listed. If the student has worked with GDP previously, the exercise list is for the lesson on which the student last worked. A ■ precedes exercises that have been completed. A ◣ precedes exercises that have been started but not completed.

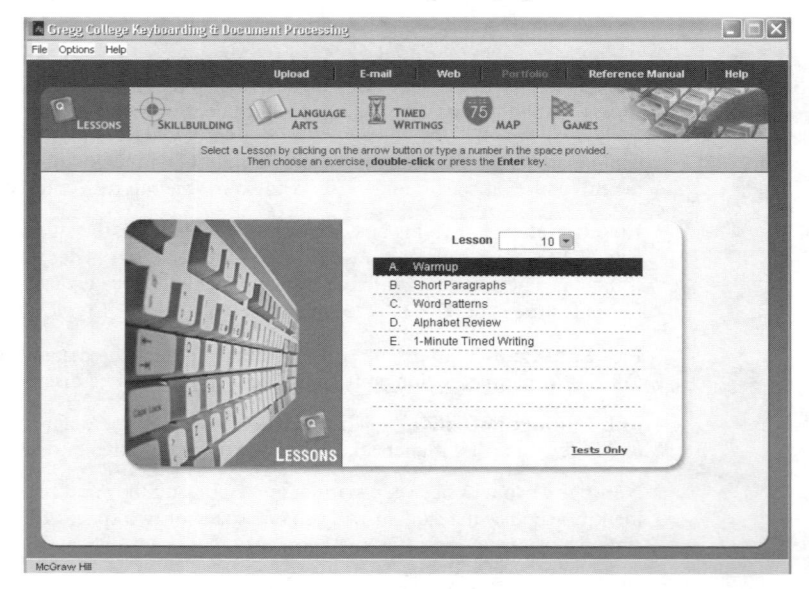

FIGURE 3-5: LESSONS MENU

To work on an exercise:

1. Select the lesson you want to open.

    - Type the lesson number into the Lesson text box.

    or

    - Open the Lesson text box by clicking the [▼] button; then scroll up or down the lesson numbers.

2. Select the exercise you want to work on.

    - Highlight the name of the exercise and press **Enter** on your keyboard.

    or
    - Double-click the name of the exercise.

3. Read the introductory or instruction screen(s) and turn to the appropriate page in the textbook. Type the text as instructed, and click the **Next** button at the bottom of the screen to go to the next screen in the exercise (For more information about the exercise screen layout, see "Exercise Screen Layout", below.).

4. When you click **Next** at the end of an exercise, GDP goes to the next exercise in the lesson. At the end of the last exercise for a particular lesson, GDP returns to the Lessons menu.

Pressing the **Esc** key allows the student to exit an exercise at any time. The student can exit the program at any point by selecting *Exit GDP* on the File menu.

3.2.1 Exercise Screen Layout

Exercise screens have the same basic layout throughout the program (see Figure 3-6).

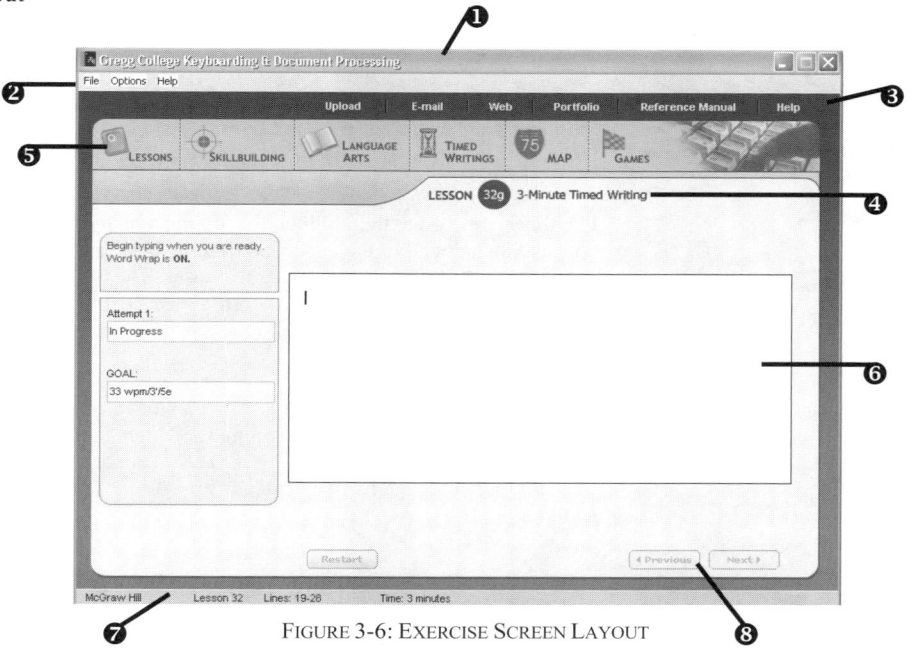

FIGURE 3-6: EXERCISE SCREEN LAYOUT

❶ **Title bar:** The title bar includes the program name and the standard window control menu (to the left) and the minimize, maximize, and close buttons (to the right).

❷ **Menu bar:** The menu bar lists all of the drop-down menus. (For more information, see "Drop-Down Menus" later in this chapter.)

❸ **Toolbar:** The toolbar includes buttons for frequently used features and on-screen guidance. (For more information, see "Toolbar" later in this chapter.)

❹ **Exercise header:** The exercise header specifies information about the current exercise, such as the speed and accuracy goals for a timing and scores on various attempts at the exercise. Goals and scores are noted as follows: number of words/number of minutes/number of errors (for example, "33wpm/3'/5e" indicates 33 words per minute for 3 minutes, with 5 errors).

❺ **Navigation menu:** The navigation menu running across the screen directly under the Toolbar includes icons for accessing GDP's activities by lesson and by activity type.

❻ **Body of the screen:** The body of the screen provides instructions or an area for typing text.

❼ **Status bar:** The status bar specifies the student's name and lesson number. Line numbers and length of a timing are indicated when applicable.

❽ **Previous and Next buttons:** These buttons in the bottom right corner of the screen are used to move sequentially through the screens in an exercise.

3.3 Navigation Menu

The navigation menu runs across every screen directly under the Toolbar, providing quick access to any activity in GDP.

Lessons — Use this icon to go to the Lessons menu. The Lessons menu displays all of the lessons and exercises in the textbook.

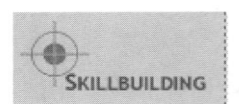

Skillbuilding — Use this icon to go to the Skillbuilding menu, which groups exercises by type and includes all of the lesson exercises except for test, language arts exercises, and document processing exercises. The Skillbuilding menu also includes Open Timed Writings, Custom Timed Writing, Supplementary Timed Writings, Numeric Keypad Practice, MAP, the Pace Car Game, and the Tennis Game, which are not accessible from the Lessons menus.

Language Arts — Use this icon to go to the Language Arts menu, which displays all of the language arts exercises in the program. The Language Arts menu provides access to language arts exercises by skill area (rather than by lesson) and includes numerous interactive language arts tutorials not found in the textbook.

Timed Writings — Use this icon to go to the Timed Writings menu, which includes all of the timed writings included in lesson exercises as well as Open Timed Writings. Custom Timed Writings, and Supplementary Timed Writings.

MAP — Use this icon to go to the MAP (Misstroke Analysis and Prescription) program, which identifies keystroking problems and prescribes remedial exercises to fix those problems.

Games — Use this icon to go to the Games menu for quick access to the Tennis Game or Pace Car Game.

3.4 Toolbar

The toolbar is a row of buttons across the top of the screen above the Navigation Menu. Use the toolbar for quick access to frequently used features and on-screen guidance. When you rest the mouse pointer over a button on the toolbar, a Tooltip shows the name of the button and the keyboard shortcut, if there is one. See "Keyboarding Shortcuts" later in this chapter.

Upload

This button, which is active in all GDP 10th Edition configurations, is used by students to send their data files to the Instructor Management Web site.

E-mail

This button is used by the student to create and send an e-mail message to the instructor.

Web

This button is used to access your campus Web site, if a URL is specified in Settings.

Portfolio

This button is used to access student reports.

Reference Manual

This button is used for help with formatting the various types of documents included in GDP.

Help

This button is used to get information about how GDP works.

3.5 Drop-Down Menus

Drop-down menus can be accessed from the menu bar running across the top of the GDP screen.

3.5.1 File Menu

Portfolio. .
Use *Portfolio. . .* to view or print a report showing the student's scores on completed GDP exercises as well as scored text for any exercise. The report can be restricted by date range, lesson number, or exercise type.

Performance Chart. . .
Use *Performance Chart. . .* to view or print a graph showing the student's speed and accuracy on all timings in a part (group of 20 lessons).

Import Student Data. . .
This feature is used to import data from one GDP location to another to allow for working on GDP in multiple locations.

Export Student Data. . .
This feature is used to create an export file of student data which can then be imported into GDP on another workstation (for example, if the student works on GDP in more than one location).

For detailed information on using the import/export feature, go to the College Keyboarding Web site at www.mhhe.gdp.com and click on the Technical Tip link.

Go to Word Processor
Use *Go to Word Processor* to link to Microsoft Word to work on documents that are not included in the textbook or print copies of completed documents without accessing those documents through the Lessons menu.

Show Announcement
The student uses *Show Announcement* to view the class announcement that you have sent to a class in a Campus with Instructor Management (LAN) configuration. If you have not posted an announcement for your class, this option is inactive. (Note that distance-learning students receive their announcements via e-mail.)

E-mail Instructor. . .
The student uses *E-mail Instructor. . .* to create and send an e-mail message to you, if you have assigned an e-mail address.

Delete Files
Use *Delete Files* to delete the student's text for selected lessons and exercise types.

✦ **Note:** When *Delete Files* is used, just the student's scored text is deleted. Scores are maintained in the student's Portfolio, but the asterisk preceding the date in the Summary Report (indicating that a Detailed Report is not available) is removed.

Exit GDP
Use *Exit GDP* to exit the program.

3.5.2 Options Menu

Personal Information...
Personal Information is used by the student to enter information such as initials, a byline, and address. GDP opens the Personal Information form when the student needs to add information.

Settings...
Settings... is used by the Home student to specify browser, word processing, and certain other settings for using GDP.

Instructor Options
Use *Instructor Options* to work with settings, set up and manage class files, use distance-learning features, look at a student's exercises and generate student grade, create Custom Timed Writings, or write comments to McGraw-Hill.

3.5.3 Help Menu

Program Overview
Use *Program Overview* for a quick text-only introduction to GDP.

Reference Manual
Use *Reference Manual* for detailed instructions on formatting the various types of documents produced in GDP.

Tutorial
Use *Tutorial* to take a short multimedia tour of the GDP program and learn how it works.

Help
Use *Help* to view the contents tab for Help topics.

Live Update (only in Home version)
Live Update is used by the Home student to see if any new updates are available for GDP10 (Note: Students will be notified automatically if this is checked off within their settings.).

About...
Use *About...* to determine which version of the program is being used. This information is useful when calling customer support.

3.6 Keyboard Shortcuts

Sometimes it is easier to use a keyboard shortcut rather than to remove your hand from the keyboard to activate the mouse. Here are the keyboard shortcuts in GDP:

Alt	**Menu Bar** Activates the menu bar.
Alt+→	**Next** Moves to the next screen in an exercise.
Alt+←	**Previous** Moves back to the previous screen in an exercise.
Ctrl+A	**Language Arts menu** Opens the Language Arts menu.
Ctrl+G	**Games menu** Opens the Games menu.
Ctrl+M	**MAP program** Opens the MAP program
Ctrl+P	**Portfolio** Provides access to student reports.
Ctrl+R	**Restart timed writing** Allows the student to restart most timed writings within the first 15 seconds.
Ctrl+S	**Skillbuilding menu** Opens the Skillbuilding menu.
Ctrl+Shft+M	**Reference Manual** Provides formatting guidelines for various types of documents.
Ctrl+T	**Timed Writings menu** Opens the Timed Writings menu.
Ctrl+X	**Exit** Exits the program. Not active within an exercise (press **Esc** to cancel the exercise first).
Esc	**Previous Menu** Cancels an exercise. If a scored exercise, the report is marked canceled.
F1	**Help** Opens Help.

3.7 Getting Distance-Learning and Standalone Student Data into Instructor Management

Students using GDP in a standalone environment—whether on campus or at home—need to provide their data files in order for you to be able to monitor their work in Instructor Management. The procedure varies according to the student's GDP configuration.

3.7.1 Sending Distance-Learning Student Data to the Instructor Management Web Site

Students using the Distance-Learning option within any of the Campus or Home configurations upload their updated student files to the Instructor Management Web site by clicking the **Upload** button on the toolbar. Before students can upload their data, however, you must register them on the Instructor Management Web site (for more information, see 2.4 Set Up the Instructor Management Web Site for Distance Learners on page 26.

At any time while logged on to GDP, the distance-learning student can send updated information to the Instructor Management Web site by clicking the **Upload** button on the toolbar. The Update dialog box then allows the student to send a complete set of data files (**Upload All Work**) or just the files the student has worked on since the previous update (**Upload Work Completed Since Your Last Update**), either by the student upload web site or via e-mail. At the end of every GDP session, the program prompts the distance-learning student to send updated work to the instructor in case the student does not send updated data during the GDP session.

3.7.2 Sending Student Data to the Instructor Management Web Site from Non-MAPI Compliant E-mail

Students who do not have MAPI-compliant e-mail can still send their data to the Instructor Management Web site. These students should install a standalone (either Campus with Instructor Management or Home) configuration of the GDP software. Students can then use the Export feature to export their work to the Instructor Management Web site. The Export feature creates a compressed file of the student's work (*.exp) that can be saved and sent as an e-mail attachment to the Instructor Management Web site using the e-mail address gdpupload@mcgraw-hill.com. The compressed file is received seamlessly by the Instructor Management Web site and the data is placed into the student's Portfolio (see 3.6.4 Sending Distance-Learning Student Data to the Instructor Management Web site in the GDP 1-120 User's Guide for information on how to transfer student data to the Instructor Management Web site).

3.7.3 Loading Standalone Student Data onto an Instructor Workstation

Students using GDP in a standalone (either Campus without Instructor Management or Home) configuration must provide their data files to you so that you can manually load them into the Instructor Management program on an instructor workstation. There are two methods for loading standalone student data into Instructor Management: by using the Update Student Data Disk File feature in the gradebook and by using the import/export feature in GDP.

Updating Student Data from Floppy Disks
If students are storing their work on floppy disks or other removable media (such as Zip disks), collect their disks and use the Instructor Management program's **Update Student Data Disk File** feature in the gradebook (available once you select **Show List of Students** in the gradebook) to copy the student data to the instructor workstation. For in-depth information, refer to Chapter 5 of the GDP User's Guide.

Importing Student Data

If students are storing their work on a fixed disk (such as the local hard drive), they can export all or part of their work to a compressed export file which you can then import into GDP onto your instructor workstation. Using the import/export feature is a three-step process:

1. The student exports his or her work and delivers it to you (on a floppy disk or via e-mail).

2. On your GDP instructor workstation, you log on to GDP *as the student* and import the student's export file.

3. Once you have imported the student's data on the instructor workstation, that data becomes accessible in the gradebook.

Detailed instructions are found in the GDP Help system.

For more information on using the import/export feature, go to the College Keyboarding Web site at www.mhhe.gdp.com and click on the Technical Tip link.

3.8 Viewing HTML Versions of Student Work

Whether or not you use GDP Instructor Management (the program or the Web site) you may want to view students work using a Web browser. The Portfolio's **Export to HTML** feature provides the ability for the student to create an HTML version of any report in the student's Portfolio.

For more detailed information on the Export to HTML feature, go to the College Keyboarding Web site at www.mhhe.gdp.com and click on the Technical Tips link.

Chapter 4: Using Instructor Options and Instructor Management

GDP Instructor Options and Instructor Management are special tools to help you make the best use of GDP.

This chapter provides a brief overview of the Instructor Options and Instructor Management. For in-depth information, refer to Chapter 5 of the GDP User's Guide.

4.1 Accessing Instructor Options

To Access Instructor Options:

1. Open the Start menu and choose Programs.

2. Point to *Irwin Keyboarding* and select *GDP Classes*.

3. The title screen displays. Select *Instructor Options* on the Options drop-down menu.

4. (When using Campus with Instructor Management configuration) Select your name from the instructor list and click **OK**. Then type **irwin!** (or your personalized password, if you changed the generic password) in the password dialog box and click **OK**.

5. (When using Campus without Instructor Management configuration) In the Instructor Options Password dialog box, type **irwin!** (or your personalized Instructor Options password, if you changed the generic password) and click **OK**.

ALERT: Keep the Instructor Options password confidential! It overrides the security provided by the software and gives access to options only the instructor should control.

The Instructor Options title screen (Figure 4-1) gives you full access to Instructor Management and other useful tools for instructors.

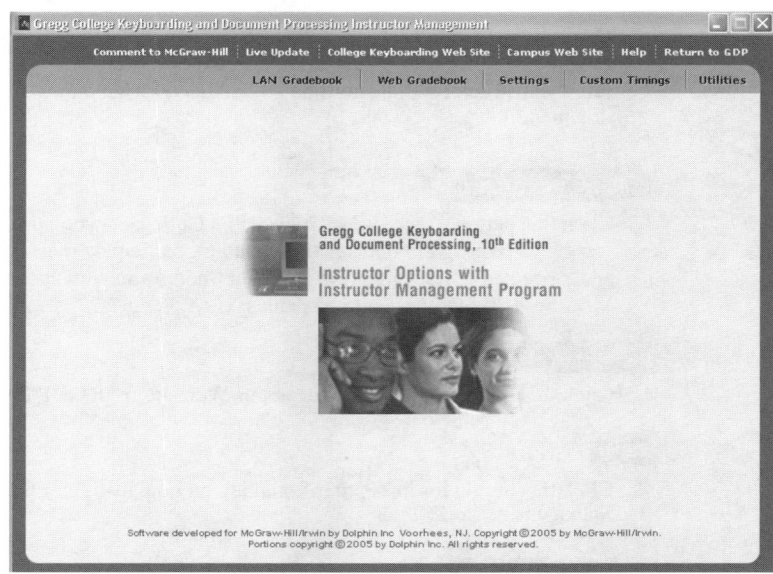

FIGURE 4-1: INSTRUCTOR OPTIONS TITLE SCREEN

Chapter 4: Using Instructor Options and Instructor Management

4.1.1 Navigation Menu

Use the navigation menu towards the top of the Instructor Options screen (underneath the Toolbar) to open the five main Instructor Options tool:

LAN Gradebook

The Instructor Management software accessible from Instructor Options provides a powerful gradebook allowing you to set up GDP classes (either on campus or for home users), record your students' scores from GDP, monitor student and class progress, and compute grades.

Web Gradebook

Clicking on **Web Gradebook** will link you to the Instructor Management Web site (IMWS). The IMWS also provides a gradebook allowing you to set up GDP classes (either on campus, or for distance-learning courses), similar to the LAN Gradebook, except students upload work via e-mail or the Student Web Site.

Settings

Global, Class, and McGraw-Hill settings give you control over certain GDP features.

Custom Timed Writings

Custom timed writings are timed writings that you create and that your students can access from the Skillbuilding and Timed Writings menus.

Utilities

Click this button if a student has sent you his or her GDP work as HTML reports and you want to verify that the student has not altered those HTML reports.

4.1.2 Toolbar

The toolbar running across the top of the Instructor Options screen gives you quick access to ancillary tools in Instructor Options.

Comment to McGraw-Hill

Click this button to open an on-screen form to report your comments, questions, or suggestions about GDP to McGraw-Hill.

Live Update

Click this button to manually check for GDP software updates that are available for download (Note: If Live Update is selected (the default) on the Instructor Settings tab, the instructor will be notified automatically when new updates are available for download.).

College Keyboarding Web Site

Click this button to access McGraw-Hill's College Keyboarding Web site, where you can get GDP program updates (if available), participate in instructor forums, read announcements from McGraw-Hill, and find information about other Irwin and McGraw-Hill products and companies.

Campus Web Site

Click this button to link to your campus Web site from GDP Instructor Options.

Help

Click this button for in-depth information on how Instructor Options and Instructor Management work.

Return to GDP

Click this button to return to GDP.

4.2 About Instructor Management (Gradebook)

For students using GDP in a Campus with Instructor Management (LAN) configuration, the Instructor Management software automatically collects student data. For students working in a standalone GDP configuration (either Campus without Instructor Management or Home (Standalone)), the instructor has to collect student data files and manually load them into Instructor Management. For students using the Distance-Learning option available within any of the three GDP configurations, they will upload their data via the student upload web site (or by e-mail as a second method) for data transfer to the Instructor Management Web site.

As referenced above, there are two versions of the Instructor Management software: the Instructor Management Web site is used in the Distance-Learning option, and the Instructor Management program is used in Campus with Instructor Management (via automatic student data collection) as well as Campus without Instructor Management and Home configurations (via manually collecting and loading student data files into Instructor Management). The features of the two versions are very similar.

To access the gradebook, click **LAN Gradebook** in the navigation menu towards the top (underneath the Toolbar) of the Instructor Options title page.

- If you are using GDP in the Campus with Instructor Management (LAN) configuration, you are now in the Instructor Management program at the Gradebook Classes page (Figure 4-2)

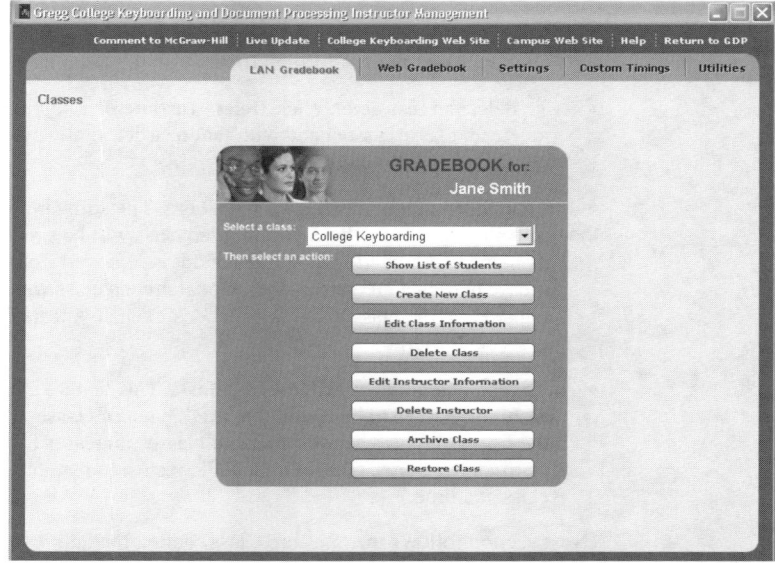

FIGURE 4-2: GRADEBOOK CLASSES PAGE IN INSTRUCTOR MANAGEMENT PROGRAM

- If you are using the Distance-Learning option available in any of the three GDP configurations, your browser launches the Instructor Management Web site and goes to the log-on page. Type your e-mail address and your Instructor Management Web site password and click **Log On** to go to the Gradebook Classes page. If this is your first time in the Instructor Management Web site, you will have to register yourself before you can use the Web site. For more information, see 2.4 Set Up the Instructor Management Web Site for Distance Learners on page 26.

✦ **Note:** The figure graphics used in this Installation Guide are from the Instructor Management program. Pages in the Instructor Management Web site generally have the same options, although the page layout is somewhat different, reflecting a Web environment.

The first screen that appears in the gradebook is the Classes page. If you have set up any classes to use GDP, they are listed in alphabetical order in the list box on this page.

4.2.1 Classes Page

- To create a new class, click **Create New Class**.

- To view the roster and grades (Classes Summary Report Page; see Figure 4-3) for the selected class or view the work of an individual student in that class, click **Show List of Students**.

- To delete the selected class, click **Delete Class**.

- In the Instructor Management program (Campus with Instructor Management (LAN) configuration), click **Edit Class Information** to change the Course/Section Name, Gradebook Selection, or Student Data Location for the selected class (Note: Once students register in the selected class, the instructor will be able to edit only the Course/Section Name field.). In the Instructor Management Web site (distance-learning option), click **Edit Class Information** to change the class name or **Manage Instructor** to change the instructor name.

(Note: the first four bullets apply to LAN Gradebook ONLY)

In the Instructor Management LAN Gradebook:

- To change the instructor name, instructor e-mail address or instructor password, click **Edit Instructor Information**.

- To delete an instructor, click **Delete Instructor** (Note: Deleting an instructor will delete all classes associated with that instructor; all students should be transferred to other classes before clicking **Yes**.).

- To archive a class, click **Archive Class**. The software will prompt the instructor to select the location where the archived class will be saved. When a class is archived, its name is removed from the list and it is removed from the total count of classes. Please note that an instructor cannot archive a class while students are actively logged into the class. (LAN Gradebook exclusive feature; you can archive only one class at a time.)

- To restore a class, click **Restore Class**. This feature allows instructors to select archived classes to be restored to GDP's list of classes. When a class is restored to the list of classes, the total count of classes increases by however many classes the instructor restores. (LAN Gradebook exclusive feature; you can restore only one class at a time.)

(Next section follows the 'Restore Class' bullet, but applies to Web Gradebook ONLY)

In the IMWS Web Gradebook, click **Manage Instructor** to:

- Change the instructor name
- Change the instructor school address
- Change the types of communication available from Irwin:

  - Receive important information and updates regarding Gregg College Keyboarding and Document Processing
  - Receive important information from McGraw-Hill

Chapter 4: Using Instructor Options and Instructor Management   51

- To delete an instructor, click **Delete Instructor** (Note: Deleting an instructor will delete all classes associated with that instructor. You can transfer each class to other instructors, or, after deleting this instructor, the students in his or her classes can be reassigned to other instructors' classes.).

- To select a different class in the LAN Gradebook, click the down-arrow button to the right of the class listed. Highlight the class you want to work with. In the Web Gradebook, select a class in the Class List and then select an option from the menu on the right.

4.2.2 Class Summary Report Page

The Class Summary Report page shows all of the students in the selected class, with component grades and a course grade for each student and average grades for the class. This page also shows the weight factors used to compute grades. (Please note that the Class Summary Report page is not the default when the instructor clicks **Show List of Students**; the default is the List of Students page, which displays all student names, student e-mail addresses, and the last date on which the student actively worked in any GDP exercise(s). To access the Class Summary Report, click on the down arrow button to the right of the "Select a report" drop-down list, and then click Class Summary Report.)

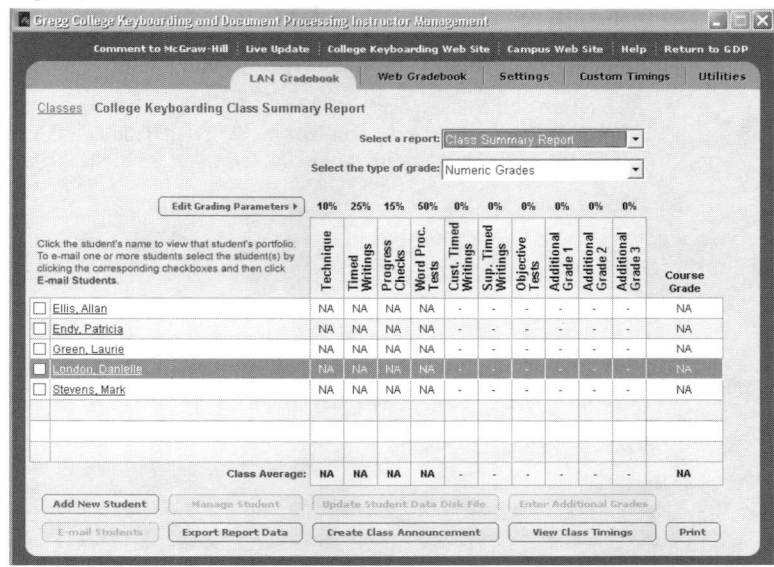

FIGURE 4-3: CLASS SUMMARY REPORT PAGE IN
INSTRUCTOR MANAGEMENT PROGRAM

- Click on the student's name to access the Portfolio (filter) Settings dialog box. Make any appropriate changes to the portfolio settings, and then click **OK** to proceed to the student's portfolio. This is where the instructor can view and print Detailed Reports, etc. (Note: To activate the **E-mail Students**, **Manage Student** and **Enter Additional Grades** buttons, select the corresponding checkbox to the left of the student's name. The instructor must check off all the appropriate student names in order to send an e-mail to multiple students; the instructor cannot manage multiple students at the same time.)

- To change a student's log-on information, transfer that student to a different class, or delete that student from the class, select the student's name and click **Manage Student**.

- If the class is set up in a standalone configuration and is storing its work on floppy disks, select the student's name and click **Update Student Data Disk File** to load updated data into the Instructor Management program. (This option is not available on the Instructor Management Web site.)

- To enter additional grades (that is, grades that are not entered automatically by GDP) for a particular student, select the student's name and click **Enter Additional Grades**.

- To add a new student to the class, click **Add New Student**.

- To compose and send an announcement to the class, click **Create Class Announcement**.

- To view a chart of timed writings for the class, click **View Class Timings**.

- To print a copy of the Class Summary Report page, click **Print** (Instructor Management program). On the Instructor Management Web site, printing is a two-step process: first click **Printer-Friendly Version** to open a new window with the print version displayed, and then click the browser's Print button to print that version of the page. Close the window to exit.

- To return to the Classes page (LAN Gradebook), click on the "Classes" link to the far left below the navigation menu. For the Web Gradebook, click on the Gradebook link within the breadcrumb trail to the left to return to the Classes Page (Gradebook).

Chapter 5: Troubleshooting

If you have any questions or problems as you install GDP or work with student data files, first make sure that your system meets the requirements outline in "System Requirements" in Chapter 1 and that you followed the exact procedure outlined in Chapter 2 for the configuration you are installing. Next, check this troubleshooting guide. If you experience a problem not covered here or not remedied by following a suggestion listed here, record exactly at what point in the program the problem occurred and a description of what happened when you or the student encountered the problem. Then call McGraw-Hill/Irwin's customer technical support at 1-800-331-5094 (8 A.M.—5P.M. CST).

5.1 Installation and Start-Up

■ **When installing GDP, the Select Destination Location dialog box indicates that the drive does not have sufficient free space.**

Explanation: GDP requires approximately 175 MB of free hard-disk space, which the selected drive does not have.

Suggestion: If you have another hard disk drive with at least 175 MB of free space, select that other drive and click **OK** to continue the GDP installation. Otherwise, press **Esc** to cancel the installation, then free up at least 175 MB of space and run the GDP installation again.

■ **When starting the program, a dialog box prompts you to insert a blank disk.**

Explanation 1: GDP has been configured to store student work on a floppy disk, and the program was started without a blank floppy disk in the floppy drive.

Suggestion: Insert a blank floppy disk in the floppy drive.

- If GDP is installed in a standalone configuration and you do not want to store student data on floppy disks, re-install GDP and specify a different student data location.

- If GDP is installed on a Campus with Instructor Management (LAN) and no students have registered into the student's class yet, you can change the student data location for the class. To do so, access Instructor Options, open the Gradebook Classes page, select the class, and click **Edit Class Information**. Then select a different option for Student Data Location and click **Save** to save your changes.

- If GDP is installed on a Campus with Instructor Management (LAN) and the student or any other classmate has already registered into the class, you cannot change the student data location. However, you can create a new class and transfer all students into the new class. See Chapter 5 of the User's Guide for detailed instructions on transferring a student to a different class.

Explanation 2: The floppy disk in unreadable.

Suggestion: Put a new, formatted floppy disk in the floppy drive.

- **When starting the program, a dialog box displays an "E003 Path not found" error message.**

  Explanation: GDP cannot find the data directory specified for student data location.

  Suggestion: If you are not using the Instructor Management program, make sure that the shortcut for the icon the student uses to start GDP includes the full path to that student's data files. If you are using the Instructor Management program, verify that the student data location is correct for the class. In either case, use Windows Explorer® to verify that student data files and directories have not been moved or deleted.

- **A Campus with Instructor Management (LAN) student is not able to access GDP when he or she previously could.**

  Explanation: You are accessing the student's work in Instructor Management while the student is trying to log on to GDP. *Suggestion:* Exit Instructor Management while your students work on GDP.

- **A Campus with Instructor Management (LAN) or Campus without Instructor Management (Standalone) student forgot his or her password and cannot get into the program.**

  Suggestion: Although you cannot view the student's original password, you can create a new one for the student in the Campus with Instructor Management (LAN) configuration. The instructor cannot create a new password for Distance-Learning students. See "Editing a Student's Log-on Information" in Chapter 5 of the GDP User's Guide.

- **For a standalone student storing data on a floppy disk, the log-on screen has another student's name.**

  Explanation: Students are not using their own floppy disks.

  Suggestion: Make sure each student starts with a new, blank floppy disk for data storage.

- **In a standalone GDP installation, launching the program from the GDP directory results in an error indicating that the program cannot find the Classes directory.**

  Explanation: The GDP program needs to know the student data location where it launches. This information is built into the program icon (shortcut) in the McGraw-Hill/Irwin Keyboarding program group.

  Suggestions: Always start GDP from the Start menu, selecting *Programs, Irwin Keyboarding*, and then the GDP program icon for the configuration you have installed (i.e., *GDP Classes, GDP Standalone,* or *GDP Home*).

5.2 Document Processing and Scoring

- **For document processing exercises, GDP fails to start the word processor.**

    Explanation: The Microsoft Word location specified on the *Instructor Settings* tab of the Settings dialog box is incorrect or it is the location for a different version of the word processor.

    Suggestion: Select *Instructor Options* on the Options drop-down menu, type the instructor password, and then click **Settings**. Select the *Instructor Settings* tab and verify the full path to your installation of Microsoft Word. For the Home configuration, select *Settings* from the Options pull-down menu to specify your location (path) and version of Word.

- **The GDP/Return to GDP menu option in Microsoft Word 2000 does not work.**

    Explanation: Templates that are added to the startup group for Word when a Hewlett-Packard printer is installed can be the cause of this problem. Hewlett-Packard adds a file so that the printer can interface with HP's By Design program.

    Suggestion: Locate the file called bs2000.dot and move it from its default location to the Templates directory.

- **A document or exercise does not get scored.**

    Explanation: The exercise is not supposed to be scored. Practice documents, warm-ups, new key presentations, and certain practices and skillbuilding and document processing exercises are not scored.

    Suggestion: If you want to score documents manually, have students print copies of their documents from within Word. If you want to score other unscored exercises manually, have students print copies of the completed exercises from their Portfolio as follows: click the **Portfolio** button on the toolbar, specify Portfolio options, click **OK** to view the Summary Report, select the exercise(s) you want printed, and click **Print Text**.

- **Scored copy contains numerous "<¶>" or "{¶}" marks.**

    Explanation: The student did not follow the word wrap setting indicated in the exercise header at the top of the screen. A "<¶>" occurs in a scored copy where word wrap is off and the student fails to press **Enter** at the end of the line. A "{¶}" occurs in a scored copy where word wrap is on and the student mistakenly pressed **Enter** at the end of the line.

    Suggestion: Retype the exercise following the word wrap setting in the exercise header.

5.3 Sound

- **No sound plays at the end of timed writings or when the restart period is over in a timed writing.**

    Explanation: GDP uses the Default Sound to signal the end of a timed writing and the end of a restart period. Your computer either has <none> (no audible sound) assigned to the Default Sound, or it has speakers attached to the computer but not turned on.

    Suggestions: First, check to make sure that the Default Sound in your Windows Sounds control panel is assigned an audible sound such as a ding, chimes, or chord. (If you are not familiar with the Sounds control panel, refer to the User's Guide for your operating system.) Also make sure that your speakers (if any are attached to your computer) are turned on and work.

5.4 E-mail

- **The *E-mail* button does not automatically appear on the Word toolbar.**

    Explanation: The **E-mail** button does not appear on the Standard toolbar. If you have not installed an e-mail program (such as Microsoft Outlook) on your computer, the **E-mail** button will not appear on the Standard toolbar.

    Suggestion: See your Microsoft Word User's Guide for additional information on the **E-mail** button.

- **The *E-mail* button does not work on the GDP toolbar.**

    Explanation 1: The system may not be configured with MAPI. When sending an e-mail, GDP uses MAPI and the system's default e-mail address.

    Suggestion: Make sure the computer uses a MAPI-compliant e-mail system and that a default e-mail address is set up. Otherwise, use e-mail outside of GDP for sending messages between instructor and students.

    Explanation 2: If the student is using GDP in a Campus with Instructor Management (LAN) configuration, the instructor may not have entered his or her e-mail address in the Settings dialog box.

    Suggestion: Access Instructor Options and open the Settings dialog box. In the Class Settings tab, enter the correct information for the Instructor's e-mail address.

    Explanation 3: If the student is using GDP Home, either the student's e-mail address or the instructor's e-mail address is missing or incorrect in the Settings dialog box.

    Suggestion: Have the student log on to the Home version of GDP, access Settings from the Options menu and enter the correct information for both the student's and instructor's e-mail addresses.

- **The *Web* button does not work on the GDP toolbar.**

    Explanation: The URL for your campus Web site is not specified in the Settings dialog box.

    Suggestion: If you are using the Campus versions, access Instructor Options, open the Settings dialog, and enter the correct URL for the campus Web site in the Instructor Settings tab. If the student is using the Home version, he or she should log on to GDP, access Settings from the Options menu, and enter the correct URL for the Campus Web site.

5.5 HELP AND REFERENCE MANUAL

■ **Clicking on the Help button or the Reference Manual button launches America Online (AOL).**

Explanation: Both the GDP Help file and the GDP Reference Manual are composed as HTML Help files. When you launch an HTML Help file, it opens in the system's default browser. If AOL is your default Internet Service Provider (ISP), it also serves as your default browser. Therefore, opening the HTML Help file or Reference Manual will also start up AOL.

Suggestion: The first time you click on Help or Reference Manual, AOL will launch, in addition to the Help or Reference Manual file. Please note that you do not need to log-on to AOL in order to use the Help or Reference Manual system. Minimize AOL to your taskbar instead of exiting the program. The next time you click on Help or Reference Manual, the file will display without also displaying AOL.

5.6 Instructor Management Program Campus with Instructor Management (LAN)

■ **The instructor cannot access a student's data in Instructor Management.**

Explanation: You are trying to access the student's work while the student is logged on to GDP.

Suggestion: Exit Instructor Management until the student has logged off GDP.

■ **Errors are encountered after the instructor uses Windows Explorer to manually move student data files.**

Explanation: It is possible that the instructor has renamed files or is mixing files from one student with those from another.

Suggestion: It is safest to move files by using the **Transfer Student** function in Instructor Management, rather than moving folders and files in Windows Explorer. If you use Windows Explorer, be sure to move the student's data folder in its entirety and do not rename the folder after you move it. The folder name containing the student's files must match the student's name on the files themselves.

5.7 Distance Learning/Instructor Management Web Site

■ **A distance-learning student is not able to upload his or her data to the Instructor Management Web site via e-mail.**

Explanation 1: Your system may not be configured with MAPI. GDP uses MAPI and the system's default e-mail address to upload data to the Instructor Management Web site. E-mail systems such as Microsoft Outlook are MAPI-compliant. AOL and CompuServe have their own e-mail systems, which are not MAPI-compliant.

Suggestion: The preferred method is to send the data via the Student Upload Web site. Click **Upload** in the top toolbar and select Upload Work to Student Upload Web site. Otherwise, either set up a MAPI-compliant e-mail system on the student's computer or reinstall GDP on the student's computer as a standalone configuration. If you reinstall GDP as a standalone configuration on a computer with a non-MAPI e-mail system, the student can export his or her work and, using his or her own e-mail system, send the export file as an e-mail attachment to the Instructor Management Web site.

Explanation 2: The student's e-mail system or the Internet connection is down or the transmission is interrupted.

Suggestion: Verify that the student's e-mail system and Internet connection are working properly outside of GDP. For example, you can have the student e-mail a message to you.

Explanation 3: The student has not been registered on the Instructor Management Web site.

Suggestion: Log onto the Instructor Management Web site, open the student's class, and verify that the student is registered into the class. The student must be registered into a class on the Instructor Management Web site before the student can upload his or her data to the Web site.

Explanation 4: The student's settings (e-mail address for the student and for the Instructor Management Web site) do not match the Instructor Management Web site settings.

Suggestion: Have the student log on to GDP and select *Settings...* from the Options menu. Verify that the student's e-mail address in the Settings dialog box matches the e-mail address for the student as it appears on the Instructor Management Web site. Also verify that the McGraw-Hill's Instructor Management Web site's e-mail address in the Settings dialog box is the correct e-mail address for the Instructor Management Web site. Have the student make necessary changes in the Settings dialog box. If the student's e-mail address is wrong on the Instructor Management Site, correct it there.

- **The student receives an e-mail stating that the GDP data was successfully received by the Instructor Management Web site, but the student data does not appear when the instructor tries to view it at the Web site.**

    Explanation: The e-mail address that identifies the student at the Instructor Management Web site is the address stored in Personal Information, which is not necessarily the address at the workstation the student uses to send data to the site. This is done so that a school administrator can setup generic e-mail addresses (e.g., workstation1@cbcc.edu) on computers in a lab and have students send data from those workstations to the Instructor Management Web site with their unique e-mail addresses embedded in the data file (e.g., student@hotmail.com).

    Suggestion: Make sure that the student's e-mail address in Personal Information (accessible from the Options menu) is the same as the e-mail address for the student at the Instructor Management Web site.

5.8 Data Storage Limits

- **A message indicates that the data disk in full.**

    Explanation: The student is about to exceed the available disk space and needs to free disk space before continuing.

    Suggestion: When this message appears, click **OK** to close the message dialog box. Exit GDP and make a copy of the full data disk, if you wish. Then, restart GDP, log-on, and select *Delete Files* on the File drop-down menu. In the Delete Files dialog box, select the lesson(s) and exercise(s) types to delete text (Detailed Reports) only. Scores for exercises with deleted text are retained on the Summary Report.

- **A message indicates that the Summary Report file is full.** *Explanation:* The maximum number of exercises that can be listed on a Summary Report is 1,000. When the Summary Report exceeds 1,000 exercises, the program automatically overwrites exercises starting with the oldest first. When this happens, you will not be able to access old exercises that are overwritten on the Summary Report.

    Suggestion: Make a copy of the data disk (or data directory), to have in case you want to access old exercises that will not be accessible when GDP is used in the future. Then continue using GDP.

Index

A

About...(Help menu), 43
Access rights, 10
Add New Student page, 27
Alt, 44
Alt+left arrow, 44
Alt+right arrow, 44
Announcement, 1, 34, 42, 48, 52
AOL, 57

B

Backing up student data files, 32
Browser, 15, 37

C

Campus Distance-Learning version, 3, 30, 38
Campus without Instructor Management (Standalone) version, 19
Campus with Instructor Management (LAN) version, 5, 6, 31, 33, 53, 54, 57
Campus without Instructor Management (Standalone) version. 3, 19, 31, 34, 45
Campus version, 2, 5
Campus Web site, 16, 48
Changing the student data location, 31
Charts and reports, 42
Class announcement, 2, 34, 42, 48, 52
Class settings, 14, 16
Classes page, 10, 50, 51
Classes subdirectory, 10, 14
Class Summary, 51, 52
College Keyboarding Web site, 48
Comments to McGraw-Hill, 48
CompuServe, 57
Create a New Class page, 27
Create a New Class dialog box, 13
Ctrl+A, 44
Ctrl+G, 44
Ctrl+L, 44
Ctrl+M, 53

Ctrl+P, 44
Ctrl+R, 44
Ctrl+S, 44
Ctrl+Shft+M, 44
Ctrl+T, 44
Ctrl+X, 44
Custom timings, 48

D

Delete Files, 42, 59
Detailed Report, 59
Distance learning, 5, 19, 27, 34, 45, 57
Document Processing, 1, 55
Drop-down menus, 42

E

Electronic Registration, 10
E-mail, 41, 42, 56, 57
E-mail address—edit, 56
E-mail Instructor..., 41, 56,
Error markings, 54
Esc key, 38, 44
Exercise screens, 39
Exit GDP, 42
Export Student Data..., 3, 42, 45, 58

F

F1, 44
File menu, 39, 42
Floppy disks, 5, 14, 17, 31, 32, 45, 52, 53, 54
Full Editing settings, 16, 17, 24, 37

G

Games menu, 40
GDP classes, 9, 31, 33, 48, 54
GDP configurations, 2, 6
Global settings, 14, 15, 16, 23, 55
Go to Word Processor, 42
Gradebook, 6, 10, 12, 13, 26, 27, 31, 45, 48, 49

H

Help, 41, 43, 46, 48, 50, 53, 57
Help button, 41, 57
Help menu, 43
Home (Standalone) version, 4, 28, 30, 36, 45
Home version, 2, 4, 5, 28, 30, 36, 56

I

Import Student Data. . ., 42
Importing student data, 45
Installation problems, 53
Installing GDP, 6, 53
Instructor Management, 1, 2, 3, 4, 5, 6, 7, 10, 11, 12, 14, 17, 18, 19, 22, 25, 26, 27, 30, 31, 32, 33, 34, 35, 42, 45, 46, 47, 48, 49, 50, 52, 53, 57, 58
Instructor Management Web site, 4, 5, 6, 18, 25, 26, 27, 30, 31, 34, 35, 45, 48, 49, 50, 52, 57, 58
Instructor Options, 11, 12, 14, 22, 23, 26, 43, 47, 48, 55, 56
Instructor Options Password dialog box, 11, 14, 23, 26
Instructor Options title screen, 47
Instructor's e-mail address, 36, 56
Instructor's workstation, 9

K

Keyboard shortcuts, 41, 44

L

Language Arts menu, 40
Lessons menu, 34, 35, 37, 38, 40
List of Students page, 27
Logging on, 33-37
Log-on password required, 15
Log-on name—edit, 54
Log-on screen, 33, 34, 36, 54

M

MAP, 1, 40, 43
MAPI, 3, 4, 28, 45, 56, 57, 58
McGraw-Hill/Irwin settings, 17, 48
McGraw-Hill's Instructor Management e-mail address, 37
Menu bar, 39, 41, 42, 44
Menus, 31-42, 44
Microsoft Outlook®, 4, 5, 28, 57
Misstroke Analysis and Prescription, 1, 40

N

Navigation menu, 39, 48, 52
Navigation menu (Instructor Options), 11, 12, 14, 22, 26, 43, 47, 48, 55, 56
Network access rights, 10
Network server installation, 10

O

Options menu, 43, 56, 58
Overview, 6, 44

P

Pace Car game, 17, 24
Password, 12, 14, 15, 22, 23, 26, 27, 47
Performance Chart. . ., 42
Personal Information. . . , 42, 58
Portfolio, 41-45, 51, 55
Portfolio button, 55
Previous/Next buttons, 39
Problems, 53-59
Program Overview, 43

R

Reference Manual, 41, 43, 44, 57
Reference Manual button, 41, 57
Required student materials, 5
Return to GDP button, 48

S

Scoring, 55
Select Class Data Location dialog box, 8, 9
Select Components dialog box, 7, 19, 20
Select Destination Location dialog box, 8, 29, 53
Select Student Data Location dialog box, 21, 29, 30
Server installation, 6-10
Setting up GDP, 6-10
Settings, 6, 14, 15, 16, 17, 22, 23, 24, 25, 29, 30, 31, 32, 45, 46, 50, 52, 48
Settings dialog box, 15, 16, 23, 24, 25, 36, 37, 56, 58
Shortcuts, 41, 44
Show Announcement, 42
Skillbuilding menu, 40, 44
Sound, 16, 24, 56
Standalone version, 45
Starting the program, 33-37, 53, 54
Status bar, 39
Student data files, 3, 5, 14, 31, 32, 49, 53
Student data storage location, 14
Student materials, 5
Student's e-mail address, 27, 28, 36, 56, 57, 58
Summary Report, 42, 51
System Requirements, 50, 53

T

Tennis game, 1, 17, 24, 40
Timings menu, 40, 44, 48
Title bar, 39
Toolbar, 14, 39, 41, 45, 48, 56
Toolbar (Instructor Options), 48
Troubleshooting, 53-59
Tutorial, 34, 35, 43

U

Updating student data, 3, 4, 5, 6, 38, 44, 54, 55, 62
Upload, 38, 41, 50
Utilities, 48

V

Virtual network connections, 14

W

Web browser, 14, 37, 46
Web button, 16, 37, 41
Windows Explorer®, 54, 57
Word®, 5, 10, 15, 36, 42, 55, 56
Word processor, 15, 23, 36, 42, 55
Word wrap, 55
Working on lesson exercises, 37-38
Workstation setup, 10

Z

Zip disks, 14, 29, 45